HypertextReview

A LITERARY ANTHOLOGY OF CONTEMPORARY WRITING

TEN YEARS AND COUNTING

D1607148

FALL 2019
VOLUME 5
CHICAGO, IL

Cover image of Diega Ortega is part of Greg Halvorsen Schreck's Las Señoras portraits. Image was created in 2019 by Greg Halvorson Schreck.

Hypertext Review
Copyright ©2019, Hypertext Magazine & Studio, Inc.

All rights reserved. No part of this publication may be reproduced or transmitted in any form or by any means, electronic or mechanical, including photocopy, recording, or any information or storage system without permission in writing from the publisher.

Hypertext Magazine & Studio, Inc.
Email: crice@hypertextmag.com

ISBN/SKU: 9781694328274

Imprint: HMS

Hypertext Review is a publication of the 501c3 nonprofit corporation Hypertext Magazine & Studio.

Find us at:
HypertextMag.com
HypertextMagazineStudio.org

Twitter: @HypertextMag
Instagram: @HypertextMag

TABLE OF CONTENTS

ESSAYS

MORE FICTION

WRITING BY HMS COMMUNITY WORKSHOP PARTICIPANTS

BREAKTHROUGH URBAN MINISTRIES

ABOVE & BEYOND FAMILY RECOVERY CENTER

BIOS

COLOPHON

Editors Note

Hypertext Magazine & Studio's Mission
We empower Chicago-area adults using storytelling techniques to give
citizens a voice and publishing to give their words a visible home.

Ten years and counting.

By reading this journal, you've already made a huge difference in both the indie lit scene and the lives of Chicago adults kicking addiction, reclaiming their lives after decades of incarceration, or recovering from chronic homelessness and poverty. How? In addition to publishing, HMS teaches Chicago-area adults to write, empowering them to tell, write and publish their own stories.

In fact, this edition is our first to include work by community members affiliated with nonprofits Above & Beyond Family Recovery Center, St. Leonard's Ministries, and Breakthrough Urban Ministries. Above & Beyond Family Recovery Center is a nonprofit that treats people with substance use disorders with "compassion, competence, and communal healing." St. Leonard's Ministries believes that "individuals want to lead productive and whole lives" and provides "a setting in which men and women recently released from prison can achieve such a life." Breakthrough Urban Ministries envisions "a safe, stable engaged East Garfield Park where success is the norm and families prosper."

This sampling of community member writing represents only a fraction of the writing our nonprofit clients produced since, when I started teaching at our nonprofit partners, I didn't properly scan clients' work or get the proper release forms signed. I've since learned my lesson!

If you're reading this, you already know the power of writing, of all forms of creative expression. That's why Hypertext's duel mission is so critical: teaching and publishing. To that end, our mission "to teach Chicago adults using storytelling techniques to give them a voice and publishing to give their words a visible home" lives online at

HypertextMag.com, in our print journal *Hypertext Review*, and through our social justice writing workshops.

Now tell me . . . how often do you see indie lit lovers and social justice pursuers together?

Since 2009, we've published thousands of professional writers and have entertained hundreds of thousands of readers online. Since 2017, our literacy programming has impacted hundreds of Chicago adults—at nonprofits including Above & Beyond Family Recovery Center, Breakthrough Urban Ministries, St. Leonard's Ministries.

It takes a pretty good-size team to address our mission of publishing and teaching. So many people have helped us along the way—the writers who trusted us with their words, the editors who have dedicated countless in-kind hours working on revisions with writers to make the story shine.

Chelsea Laine Wells, your boundless talent, energy, and support has truly sustained this endeavor.

To our senior editors Karen Halvorsen Schreck, Brian Schlender, and Amy Crumbaugh, your sharp eyes, good sense, and dedication fuel the online journal. Thanks to One Question editor Sarah Mulroe for your work on this important feature and to our typesetter extraordinaire Celeste Paed. As always, huge gratitude to our copyeditor and all-around-publishing guru Linda Naslund. Thanks to Greg Halvorsen Schreck and Diega Ortega for allowing us to use the image that appears on our cover.

Thank you to our current and former board of directors. None of this would be possible without you.

Huge gratitude to our generous HMS donors. Their support has truly made our mission possible.

HMS DONORS

Maija Rothenberg
Garnett Kilberg Cohen
Kristine Kinder
Rita Dragonette
Peggy Shinner
Mitsuko & Randy Richardson
Cyn Vargas
Ben & Debra Tanzer
Janet Joseph
Vesna Neskow
Gail Wallace Bozzano

Linda Joseph
Kathleen Quigley
Anonymous
Ceci Fano
Duff Lindsay
Tracy Boychuk
Kim Clancy
Betsy Hoying
Phil & Coleen Joseph
Tony Bowers
Christine Sneed
Patricia McNair

Carrie & Matt Feldman
Sam & Michelle Tanios
Debbie Morello
Keidra Chaney
Matt Covert
Elaine Soloway
Hank Tanzer
Julia Bocherts
Maggie Manoyan
Khloe U. Karova

Susan S. Meier
Phyllis Medrano
Bryanna Tartt
Terry Hiner
Viki Gonia
Terry Adams
Terry Clark
Randall Albers
Tom Fate
Bob & Amy
  Dixon-Kolar
Lani Montreal
Karin Evans
Julia Poole
Pamela Parker

Karen & Greg
  Halvorsen Schreck
Eve Connell
Larry Rosenthal
Cyn Vargas
Randi Woodworth
Ola Faleti
Anonymous
Joanne Hollatz
Chelsea Laine Wells
Peggy A. Wagener
Sadie M. Maul
Samantha Hoffman
Kevin Koperski
Roberta Richardson

Meddie Rodriguez
Kim Strickland
Kim Korhonen
Jill Schoeneman-
  Parker
Christina Rodriguez
Patrick Salem
Ceci Fano
Duff Lindsay
Cindy Specht
James Twist
Amy Smith
Susan Wooten
Mary Markis
Allison Bacon
Joseph Heringlake

Finally, thanks to the writers who have trusted us with their words. To find out more about Hypertext Magazine & Studio or to donate, visit HypertextMagazineStudio.org. And if you're not already reading *HypertextMag.com*, check that out too.

Christine Rice, Founder & Editor

Hypertext Magazine & Studio Board of Directors

Tony Bowers
Eve Connell
Greg Gerding
Karen Halvorsen Schreck
Janet Joseph
Chelsea Laine Wells
Ben Tanzer
Cyn Vargas

Board of Director Alums

Randy Richardson
Vesna Neskow
Sheree Greer

Homage to Akilah

Ana Castillo

*(For Akilah Oliver
and Oluchi, en memorium)*

His body was decomposing   her baby   her flesh   child she once held
at her breast. *(He was dead.)*
 Death took residence   in her head.
Neglect. Negligence. Hospital sued
over a young man left in an emergency room.

                                                                                Mine,

was incarcerated.
How was it   all became a crap shoot,
fate of offspring   we'd nourished, adored,
gave to our last breath? They--our babies   girls   boys
 muchachitos   *niños queridos*
neighborhood kids—pudgy or puny and picked on
or had too many *tíos,*
Los García or the Walkers   mom had Lupus or *marido* with
bad back & couldn't work.   Nephews nieces *mijos   mijas*
nietos   nietas   sent out to the war on streets
society wouldn't let them be,

not last century or the one before   and not in 2018.

A poet   woman   mother   raised a boy
migrant teacher of language   went from campus to campus;
plethora of words in her arsenal   Akilah and me, tokens--
brown   female   evolved spirit
from the Southwest or Southside of any city.
She was a teacher with dreads and sleepy-eyed smile   believed—
must have--in doing right doing it strong   for the sake of
teaching her son right from wrong.
If you stayed steady, she said to herself (must have)
captain on a ship of two, where *Ramen* noodles or mac n cheese dinner,
night bath regular, a story read, put the child to bed
graded papers 'til 2 a.m., then started again (must have, like I had)
the child
you raised
 would benefit   fly like Obama had. Success—
at his fingertips.
No one would shoot him down in a gated community,
No policeman would kill him dead for reaching into a pocket,
No school would hold him back 'til he gave up.
Diabetes and other diseases would be kept at bay.
He'd be ready   your boy   your flesh.   your son (& mine)
mi'jos
for the perpetual onslaught.

The time came for round one   bell rung   Oluchi,   fists up,
graffiti can,
the newly minted Black man fell.   Just like that.
Just like that.

When she got the call, ran down to MLK Hospital,

put her ear next to his lips--

bloated and bluish, parched like onion skin,

having kissed their last-kiss lips, swollen and soundless,

felt no breath,

 heard no final "Mama, I love you,"   Her boy

left to perish on a gurney

                          her son her flesh,

she started to die, too, right then.

Slow drip of existence oozed through her pores.
Good-bye, love.,
Good-bye, far-reaching star,

order a round of green mint tea for the house before we move on.
Joy, as she once knew it, vaporized.

I felt it way 'cross the land   of the free and the brave

(belonging to Whites with money and no conscience.) In a world

le monde un mundo   where no education,

knowledge of couplets, art, or science,

extent of good works,

community service,

lectures attended or charitable donations,

would re-set a heart broken

by a child's ruin.

                                        I'll testify

not knowing each other

but the way soldiers instantly bonded.

I heard her wail

like a canine hears a dog whistle, ears up, heart pounding.

We'd shared the vanity of affording good nutrition,

books, clean water and little league.

Nothing had saved them,

not us—Amazon mothers.
(Somehow, I'll say it now,
men, their own kind, had failed them—

abandoned the cause, went on to other households, other children.)

One afternoon, standing in her living room,

tired of beating without his, Akilah's heart stopped.

She hit the rug heavy,

sun filtering through bay windows

kept her lifeless body warm 'til they found her.

The killing fields are everywhere

on the train   bus   bike   work   gym or club.

Chicago   L.A.   Denver   New York.

Mothers. aunts   lil sis   *abuelas*

with outlined lips & swaying hips--

single mothers push grocery carts on the sidewalk,

sneak out to dance,

fuck in alleyways hoping for love again,

stretch meals through the week,

 have pre-paid phone cards,

spend paychecks in advance—

survive in the cracks.

I'd taught him to tie his shoes,

later, his tie, shave, ride a bike, drive a car,

have pride in work, clean the house, fry an egg, wash out his drawers,

be respectful of women, neighbors, be an honorable friend.

Now, I said to him by mail:

Look at this poet.

Look at her life,

Look at mine, see your own.

Look at her son's wall art,

know he died at 21.

Mi'jo, don't die there.
Don't leave your mother
out here

alone.

Epilogue:

Mi'jo returned

& I did not end like Anticlea in hell.

Whitman

Ana Castillo

I imagine him lying on his back,
gaze to the azure sky, white clouds—unlike
this grey New York on a rain-drenched day.
Notebook at his side, sheets splotched from an ink pen;
pipe in hand, hat off, wispy hair rustling in the wind.
Leaning on an elbow over wet dandelions he slaps
at a buzzing fly. The poet reaches for language
until evening falls.
                    At last, he stands,
dusts off trousers and heads for the pub. After an ale or two,
 "Come to me," he'll whisper to a ginger haired mate,
"when the gaslights grow dim."
That was that, life, not fate.

Walking home, pondering the vastness of an indigo sky
the poet falls in love,
the way old men fell in love, with unspoken desires

and hearts that broke into clusters of stars,
winked back at a bespectacled stare with failing sight.

Illuminated streets were new.
Everything gleamed with the shine of progress,
railways and motor cars—
democracy in action. The nation belonged to men of ambition,
ladies and their heirs. He, with his rhyme-less verses pertained to no one,
 or so he rigorously declared.
On a fair day, the friend and he hiked through the woods,
vigorous in intent, thought and perseverance.
They had wine and bread, clever banter.
Perhaps, they swam in the river.
 While their flesh dried in the sun, one read to the other.
On such days the poet felt alive again,
the feeling a treasure to store with saved letters,
scraps of new, memories of youth.
That way he'd remain immortal,
virile in the minds of romantics.

Rhetorical questions were for lesser minds.
The poet would be the one to ask.
True pleasure was soup served out of the kettle.
He'd killed the turkey or duck, twisted its neck,
plucked feathers, pulled out liver and gizzards.
Heart dropped on his own tongue, raw.
Everything else went into the boiling pot.
Later, meat melting off the bone,
potatoes, carrots and love, sweet and warm,
the poet called out, "It's done!"

MyFirst Cancer Poem

Ana Castillo

Feet forward.
Head faces technician.
Clamp comes down   presses hard. They were
lovely, some said,
a pair of violent lotuses rising from a pond,
my brown existence.   I was young,
luscious, some said.
How many women (and men) paid good money
 for such benefits? Some asked.
I laughed (as we do taking a gift for granted.)

The premature infant was nurtured on those breasts.

Lay flat, face down, Ma'am.
Let the breast hang through the opening.
(Something pushes down, sharp cut. Later,
confirmation.)

I saved my own life, the surgeon said,

having a routine exam. She left most of what now

I no longer show off.

Pain,

constant.

Bone density and memory losses last.

 I celebrate each birthday, every anniversary counts.

Time moves on.

.

Five years pass,

new dull throb,

 same breast.

Feet forward.

Head faces technician.

Down comes the clamp.
Take a seat,

Wait. We'll call you. Wait.

 Have a nice rest of your day, Ma'am.
Go home now. Wait.
 Don't think of what.
Water the crocuses. Make dinner plans.
 Take deep breaths, Stay cognizant of how easy they come today.

Embroidery

Fleda Brown

You will not perhaps believe this but I embroidered
pillowcases with the initial of my intended, when I was 16.

You have to separate the strands to get the tiny lines,
you have to circle back and back for the chain stitch.

You have to maintain a certain tautness. You have to sit
like an old lady by the fire. You are as ancient as Cro-Magnon.

There are embroidery fossils from 30,000 BC. Chinese thread-
work from 3500 B.C. You do this if you want to knot yourself

to the ages. There is chain stitch, stem stitch, that looks like
rope, split stitch (needle up through the middle) running

stitch, like a dotted line. Flame out, you skies, while
the stitches hold a filigree of vines! *Filigree*, from the Latin

for thread, and grain, grain turned into embellishment.
And curlicues, for the way longings can turn on themselves

as if they were confined to a closet. Think of Emily Dickinson
sewing one fascicle of her poems to another with a chain stitch.

Think of her, bent, birdlike, dipping and pecking.
Someone in China has machine-embroidered Klimt's *The Kiss*

with gilt threads. Such devotion to detail. An artist named Ana
has embroidered rivers, moss, and rocks, falling loose,

outside the frame, off the hoop. Ana of the twenty-first century!
Try to imagine my young finger, unwrinkled, positively dewy,

thimble-capped, driving the needle through the dotted line.

Flying Through a Hole in the Storm

Fleda Brown

The plane shudders and shakes and lurches.
Outside, lightning, exposed and buried by clouds.
The lady next to you has a dying sister,
and takeoff was long delayed, and you don't ask
if it might be too late. You are thinking
of the German plane crashed in the Alps by the co-pilot
who wanted to die and take everyone with him
and you're thinking how living is always lit against
the dark and you think there I go again making
metaphor while the lady sits there while lightning
connects the plus at the top of the cloud
with the minus at the bottom as if the cloud were
at war with itself, driving itself crazy trying to reconcile.
You have a sense of flying through space
which is funny because you always are, as surely
as if you were Saint Francis flapping your habit
down the road, keeping nothing, giving away even
what you need, smiling at the lack, the beautiful
emptiness that allows birds to fly through, even
through clouds, and allows for the forest
to be clothed for its creatures and you one
of its creatures with bare feet and the kind of
attention that can turn to the lady, shedding
everything else. You see Saint Francis and his monks
heading down the road, joyful and homeless.

You feel the attraction of homelessness
to those with homes, the wish to be free,
to be weightless, but always as an in-between
state, with a fire someplace, a hearth, a sister.
Still, the mind doesn't shake it off, the plane not
arriving, heaven not coming on earth, and
what it must look like from out there at night,
this lone vessel carrying on with its small lights.

Stalking the Wild

Fleda Brown

You should have seen us scooching from the car
with our walkers, me from knee surgery, him
from the accumulations: the back, the hips.
By you I don't mean anyone in particular, only
the you that means someone should be witness
to what happens! Witness to the tender return,
the determined positioning, the elevator ride.
Who would have thought, is another way to say it.
No high drama, no wailing wall, only the slow-
burning aches that bear our names and ride
to the third floor, where we head toward the door,
leaning like two pigeons caught in a wind, greeted
by Wally the cat on his back, his expanse of white
belly waiting to be rubbed if we could reach
down far enough. We both wish to inform you
that the situation has become absurd, absurd!
Surely you recall, we wish you to recall, Tarzan
and Jane calling out across the vines. Wild animal
thrills! Johnny Weissmuller, lock of hair across
his brow like an impulsive boy's. Cavalier.
Who doesn't love cavalier, and what lies under it,
the lone, the arch presentation? We'd like to
see you try it, yourself, with your two hands
on the walker's handles! Watching to lift over
the dangerous oriental rug. Witness, now,

as your eyes must adjust to a fainter light, what
you're in for: the unexplored, the ruins,
the behemoth and leviathan. Good God, the cooling
of magma beneath the forest floor, the mad
crack in the earth's mantle, and the small triangle
of the rug's corner caught like a lapping tongue.

Immigrant Grasses

Mike Puican

Words, overheard
in garden shops,
        uptown and earnest,
blossom into cablegrams

        from South Korea
or Cameroon; oleander,
        unscented blue star,
becomes

        a refugee
from a royal Malaysian family
        exhausted
from her long ocean voyage;

        gladioli, pale-green
and unblossomed,
        in uncertain translation,
become voluminous

        and blood-red;
common yellow snapdragons
        conjure
the emblazoned railway

                embankments
of Bucharest.
                Radiant,
reassembled, worlds

                arise from colonnades
of cosmos,
                from nasturtium
and bloodroot

                reshaped on someone's
traveled tongue:
                alyssum
of untold losses,

                immigrant grasses
rising between
                the floorboards.
Unsettled

                and urgent: these
images created by
                gardeners
and railway conductors,

                shipbuilders and
fruit polishers,
                nurturers whose
worlds crest,

                broad-leafed
and crimsoned, whose words
                offer the chance
to grow fluent in

                something
that has no concern
                over what meanings
are indigenous.

Sunset at a Lake

Mike Puican

A woman sings to her daughter

in the grass; a teenager

    argues   with her boyfriend

  on a cellphone; an air conditioner

       shudders

    from a snack shop on the beach.

Three men watch two TVs in the shade.

Sweat bees circle

    their beer cans.   A five-year-old

squeals from the top of Sheridan's horse.

       The sun moves

    in slow increments of dying.

A phone line cuts the sky like a

closed eye.

      Mars brightens   as dusk

  twists its way into a heart.

                  A mosquito pulls

  from my arm until full.

Red Line

Mike Puican

Knife slicing the living night,
nacreous river, we've stood waiting for you
many times before. And still we wait.

River of departure, arrival, departure.
Container of all ambition, you make us
what we are: employable, fuckable.

Night-blue finger tracing the lake's shore,
airstream of avarice and hearts askew,
carved into the suddenly valuable land

of broken-down homes and buried
children. Our hopes, our bodies fill you,
conductor, with metal cheeks,

200-watt eyes offering glimpses
of bedrooms, over-stuffed chairs and
their punishments, storefronts

lit like flames. You carry day traders
dressed for sentencing, mothers
working on resumes, outcasts

busking for change. In your care,
a steady ticking, the learned comfort of metal
on metal, the caress of night feathers.

O snake among the roses, we
await your approach, the cold snap
of doors flung wide open.

Portrait as Landscape: No longer fragment or trace

Simone Muench & Jackie K. White

I used to wear an autumn face and drape
myself in taupes, in grays. I was leaf shriveled,
water-logged, the open mouth of a vase
gone murky, its shatter and strew. I used

to swear a frayed array of sadnesses
in several slangs that everyone ignored
until a snow squall caught one syllable—
timbred with a spell, a prayer, a curse?—

that shot me to a center, whole, sun-flared
and spinning loose from that pinned darkness.
No longer echo or contour, but full-throated,

spring-fresh unfolded in every budding hue.
No longer fractured or lax, but limb sure
and language? Lush, languid, lean and heard.

Recast

Simone Muench & Jackie K. White

Loss enters stage left in the form of violins
thrumming the past into forecast: mulberries
in the backyard, first time, a cushioned mess
of mauve stain, caress and bruise, then forgivings.

Loss is a severed finger sent spinning
into the lake, the sun magnifying
a ring's opal fire and its milky insistence
that we break everything we love, the way

I broke apart the carnation corsage,
the way you broke my bargaining lips
on the belt buckle gift. A guitar meant

for crooning becomes a life untuned,
a molded fruit. We can't recast ruin.
We have to sit in the taint. Survive it.

Dear Dark Garden

Simone Muench & Jackie K. White

Outside, lining the hushed cul-de-sac,
dogwood white and pink blossoms peak
to petal cascades hiding more basement
girl-held horrors. The pastoral not speaking

of rot. The suburban silent about ruin.
But the girls speak—of shatter, of strangle.
Of broken teeth, of more danger. The body
bent acutely into shame. *Dear dark garden*

where you buried me, where you watched my bare
feet slipping, his ropy arms grabbing, his full
body falling on my trunk, breaking limbs
with an inarticulate hiss, say now how I was

blackened under crush of shovel and loam.
Backyard afterlife, a new rage, an old, old wrong.

Self-Portrait Lined with Wallace Stevens

Simone Muench & Jackie K. White

When sickness comes, when disease, when
a dirty house in a gutted world finds us deserted,

our bodies deflated narratives, our voices re-pitched,
we turn to libraries to fling our stalled frames forward

into covers, into jackets, into comfort and into solid,
but there's no fit, and the story can't be rewritten.

When we *feel it breathing there*—this illness, this odd
other, both bookmark and bridle—churning its sourness

through our lungs, whose words, what spell can
we exhale? What language-medicine could expel

this hex hovering in our flesh, this foul insertion
in our cellular record? Here's a missive to our harm,

a written reminder that we will refurbish what's been
dented or dimmed: Dear body-bruised, we will breathe in

our brokenness, fill in the cracks with gold, with *the pale
light that each upon the other throws.*

Portrait as Landscape: In this grim play

Simone Muench & Jackie K. White

Listen to the wilderness as it sighs
under its forest of bones. So many
beings buried here: carcasses licked
back to bare anatomy. So many

epithelial cells shed: forearms, thighs,
the brush or scratch from human or tree
or sting. So many silences, a voice crypt
sky-wide or swamp-deep. Still not enough

forewarning in this grim play. The chronic
coldness of this grove is a composite
of moss, fox, rot. Listen to its articulations

as they accordion a history, a litany of the frail
we failed to help unfold into fierceness.
So many bright flowerings forfeited.

Blue Flower Tattoo

Lillie M. Rice

It was a blue flower
What kind of flower?
A blue one
On her hand
On the top
It was colored in
It was tattooed on the ship
Came over from Lebanon to Canada
They had nothing to do
It was a blue flower
They tattooed it right onto the back
Who?
Of her hand
A blue flower
Just here
She points
Draws it with her finger
My grandma can't hear very well
And I can see her hand
Just as her mother's was
Olive and wrinkly
And bony
Fragmented conversations about hands
And flowers and tattoos
A blue flower on a bony hand
A good luck charm into a new life

The Devil in the Details

John McNally

Part One

It was the last thing on Mary Flynn's mind when she crawled into bed that night, but by the time she closed her eyes for sleep, the overwhelming lure of sin had wrapped itself around her neck, as comforting as a scarf.

The year was 1853. Mary was ten years old, a little girl in a small southern Illinois town, and each night, before blowing out the candle in her room, her father told her a story from the Bible.

"Adam named me serpent, so serpent I shall be," her father had begun tonight. "I watched Adam name every beast of the field, the cattle and the fowl, and then the next day I watched Eve form of Adam's rib, and I thought, *she's mine.*" He reached out and pinched Mary in the area of her ribs, and she squealed.

The entire time her father spoke, Mary imagined the snake speaking directly to her. Was the snake smiling? Yes. Well, sort of. All snakes smiled, more or less. But this snake was meeting Mary's eyes as it spoke and slithered closer.

Her father concluded, "And that's when I saw something in Eve I had not seen before, something that made me want to slither from a branch and onto her arm, and then slither from her arm to her breasts, and then wrap my cold flesh against her warm flesh, tightening ever so

---

This is an excerpt of John McNally's "The Devil in the Details." To read the full story, visit http://hypertextmag.com/

gently so as to feel her against me, the two of us one flesh, as she had been with Adam. I saw it in her eyes, how she would enjoy this, and then she reached for the fruit and plucked it from its stem."

Her father set his black cowboy hat atop his head and then put his lips close to the flame, so close Mary was certain he was going to burn them, and then he smiled and blew gently, allowing the flame to flicker and grow before he blew harder. The room went dark.

Her father, the Sheriff, extinguished lives in much the same manner. He would tell a story to the gathering crowd while the criminal stood with a noose around his neck, wrists tied behind his back, and rope so tight around his ankles so that the condemned man had to be carried to his final destination. A balled-up kerchief would be stuffed inside the criminal's mouth. It was too late for pleas, her father reasoned, and he certainly didn't want to be interrupted while telling the crowd a story, sometimes the same story he'd told Mary the night before—the story of Sodom and Gomorrah, or the story of Abraham giving his son Isaac back to God, or, as tonight, the story of the serpent and the Tree of Knowledge.

"Do not take advantage of a widow or an orphan," he yelled last week from the gallows, quoting from memory. "If you do and they cry out to me, I will certainly hear their cry. My anger will be aroused, and I will kill you with the sword. Your wives will become widows and your children fatherless."

He stood by the lever that opened the trapdoor, but instead of simply pulling it, he waited until the crowd had worked itself into a lather—the wronged party yelling for the lever to be pulled, the condemned man's family begging for mercy.

At her father's request, Mary had gathered as many of her classmates as she could find, and they called out for the Sheriff to pull the lever, parroting the adults beside them. And then, finally, her father pulled the wooden stick, the floor below the criminal's bound feet opened, and the crowd fell silent as the condemned man's neck snapped. The dead man's family wailed loudly, running to the gallows before deputies could cut the body down.

The candle's been blown out, Mary thought upon seeing the dead man. Smiling, she shut her eyes.

Until she was ten years old, Mary held a prestigious and much-envied position among her classmates as the daughter of the town's sheriff, but then the cold wind blew and a shift occurred. Most of the adults in town remained at home during the executions, and once some of them found out that Mary had been luring their children to these displays, they openly criticized her for what she was doing.

"You're an evil little girl," they told her while other parents clutched their children closer whenever Mary appeared in the town square, as though she were capable of the most heinous acts.

Mary still had her friends, but once word circulated that she was an evil girl, it eventually penetrated her inner circle. One by one, the girls dropped away until one day Mary found herself all alone.

And then came the snake.

For as long as Mary could remember, she'd always walked to school with her friends, cutting through acres of woods together, using a path that had come about from years of use as a shortcut. The rest of the woods flourished, a dense patch of bizarre weeds, some poisonous to the touch, and vines that slowly strangled whatever they had seductively wrapped themselves around. There were dozens of fallen trees, leafless and gray, including one large tree lying across their path, requiring the children to climb over it each morning, risking a torn dress or skinned knee.

After rumors of Mary's wickedness took root and spread, her friends stayed several yards ahead of her, as though they didn't know her, picking up their pace even as she called out for them to slow down.

"*Please*," she whined. "I can't walk as fast as you in these shoes. *Please* slow down."

Her friends, speaking amongst themselves, acted as though they hadn't heard her. Only Rachel, the last friend that still talked to Mary, waved her arm and called out, "Hurry up, Mary! We can't wait for you!"

It was an unseasonably hot May morning. Mary attempted to cross the fallen tree, but before she could swing herself over the trunk, her left leg snagged on something. It burned, too—a searing hot pain. She attempted to detach her leg from whatever had taken hold, but her leg barely budged. The pain grew sharper, her leg hotter. When she finally looked down, she saw that a cottonmouth had sunk its fangs into her calf and wasn't letting go. It had come from the nearby Big Muddy River, no doubt, out of which snakes slithered every fall, searching for cracks and crevices to burrow for the winter.

Mary almost fainted at the sight of the snake, but she held on long enough to shriek for help.

"A snake's got me! Please come back!"

But the girls walked faster, rounding a bend and disappearing from Mary's view. They never even looked back.

Mary slid off the tree and tried running home, hoping the snake would let go of her, but the snake held on, and Mary's progress was excruciatingly slow. She was barely able to move the leg that was being bitten. When she looked behind her and saw that the snake was longer than she was tall, she fell to her knees. She felt as though she were swimming through the woods, each wave of bark and stone growing darker than the last, until everything turned black.

What Mary saw when she opened her eyes was an old man's lips pressing tightly against her bare leg. First, she screamed and tried wriggling away, but the man, keeping his lips firmly in place, looked up at her, and his eyes told the whole story: *Don't move…I'm saving your life.*

And this was, in fact, what he was doing. He was sucking the venom from her leg. He would suck then spit, and then he would suck some more. When he was done sucking out the venom, he stood and lifted Mary up into the air, draping her over his shoulder, as though she were a sack of grain, and began walking into town. He didn't speak. He was as old as her grandfather but stronger than anyone she knew, except for maybe her father. He picked up his pace.

"Am I going to die?" Mary asked the man carrying her.

The man didn't answer.

He carried her to Dr. Merchant's front door and kicked with his foot. The doctor himself opened the door but took a step back at the sight of the man.

"What did you do to her?" Dr. Merchant asked.

"Snake bite on the leg," the man said. "Big one." He handed the girl over and said, "I seen to sucking out the poison."

"Okay then," the doctor said. "You can go now."

The old man regarded Mary in the doctor's arms. He tried to touch Mary's head, as though to say, "You'll be all right," but the doctor stepped back and said, "Go on now. I've got work to do." The doctor carried Mary into another room, shutting the door between her and the man who had saved her life. The doctor said, "I don't know who's got more evil in him—the snake that bit you or that old man." He set Mary down atop an examination table and said, "Let's see your leg now, dear."

The old man, it turned out, was Phineas T. Rider. Rumor was that Phineas had murdered a child twenty years earlier, and although he'd been found not guilty—the child's broken neck and head injury were blamed on a fall from Phineas' hayloft—there were some in town who maintained that Phineas, a mysterious character who lived alone, was somehow responsible. A year after the child's death, Phineas further isolated himself, rarely coming to town. His house, choked by weeds, had started to look like a natural part of the Earth itself, a berm of vines and moss, according to the few people who claimed to have seen it. Until the day he carried Mary to the doctor's front door, it had been two years since anyone had laid eyes on him. Many people had just assumed the old man had died, but no one had bothered to follow up on their conjecture.

Upon learning that Phineas T. Rider had saved his daughter's life, the Sheriff said, "Whether that child died by his hand all those years ago or not, he's square with me. His debt's been paid." On other occasions, the Sheriff said, "I never did believe he'd killed that child. You can't keep twenty-four watch over your own hayloft, now can you?" Weeks after the snake bite occurred, the Sheriff said, "I should pay the old man a visit. To offer my thanks." But he never did.

Mary saw how easily it could happen—the accusation followed by isolation—because she had seen it happen to herself. She also saw how the old man's act of saving her was his way to set things right with the townsfolk. Her father called it redemption.

"Some men eventually redeem themselves. Others are incapable of it," he said. "Those are the ones we hang."

As her leg healed, she spent a good deal of time thinking about Phineas T. Rider. What did he do all day? What did his house really look like? Was there anyone—anyone at all—to whom he spoke regularly?

When she was ready to go back to school, she decided to look for Phineas's house on her walk through the woods. The few friends who had been with her the day of the snakebite no longer spoke to her, leaving her to walk through the woods alone, which was fine: they certainly wouldn't have understood Mary's fascination with a man who had been accused of murdering a child.

During that first week, as hard as she tried, she couldn't see anything that resembled a house. But then she had an idea. She waited until a cool night and then walked to the highest elevation in town, which she had already staked out, and from this vantage point she peered out over the woods looking for evidence of Phineas's house. And sure enough she found a thin twist of smoke deep in the woods. From the best she could determine, the house was located closer to the south part of the woods, where no path could be found. She would have to fight her way through weeds and fallen trees, risking more snakes and God only knew what else, but seeing where Phineas lived had become more than just idle curiosity: it had become a chance to glimpse her own future. *This could be me*, she mused.

The next morning, Mary set off to find the old man.

Before she could veer off the path toward where she believed Phineas lived, a group of boys and girls stood waiting for her by the fallen tree.

Andrew White was a fat boy whose double chin waddled when he turned his head, and until this moment, Mary didn't even realize that Andrew had any friends. He stepped out from the whispering assembly and said, "Let's see it."

"Let's see *what*, Andrew?" Mary said. She grinned defiantly, expecting those who normally would have spoken ill of Andrew White to smile along with her, but all eyes remained on Andrew, who held some heretofore unseen power over her old friends.

"Let's see the mark on your leg," Andrew demanded. He was holding a Bible. Mary saw that now. Andrew's father was a minister with a tiny church in the deep woods, but Mary had never met anyone who worshipped there.

"We're going to be late for school," a girl behind Andrew complained. Mary had assumed the complaint was leveled at Andrew for making this silly request, but then the girl said, "Come on, Mary. We're not playing. Do what Andrew tells you to do."

Mary took a deep breath. Sensing the mood had shifted, Mary began to shiver. "Okay then," she said, and she hiked up her skirt to reveal the two still-crimson fang marks. The skin around the marks was as puffy as a snake's throat.

Andrew White moved closer to examine Mary's leg. The other children formed a circle around her, as though they'd rehearsed this moment. Andrew knelt down, set the Bible on the dirt, and took Mary's leg in both hands, the way he might hold a small, valuable statue. While on his knees, he peered up at Mary once, and she remembered dragging the long snake behind her, barely able to move her leg at all. A chill ran up through her.

Andrew picked up his Bible, stood, brushed off his knees, and walked backwards, until he had reached the circle of Mary's former friends. He raised his Bible in the air and shook it while pointing at Mary's leg with his free hand.

"Behold!" he yelled. "The mark of the beast!"

Mary opened her mouth to laugh, but the other children reached into their satchels, removed various objects, and began throwing what they held at Mary. Mary didn't move at first, frozen in place as her head, torso, and legs were hit with old, hardened bread, a ball of twine, a piece of fruit. But then, as more things hit her, she screamed and crouched, yelling for them to stop.

"Satan lives among us!" Andrew called out.

Small pebbles, a pencil, and an apple core struck Mary. A clump of dirt exploded against her ear, causing her to tip over onto her side and clutch her head.

When Phineas T. Rider stepped out from the woods, the children scattered, all except for Andrew White. Andrew held the Bible up to Phineas and said, "Are you going to kill me, too?" He asked this without fear. It was more of a challenge, a dare, but Phineas ignored Andrew, scooping Mary off the ground and carrying her safely away, into the woods.

"You and me," Phineas said as he carried Mary, "we're the same."

Mary had her arms around Phineas' neck. She was shivering and sniffling.

"How did you know I needed help?" she asked.

"I din't," he said. "Two times you been where I walk. Same place."

"They said I had the mark of the beast," Mary said.

Phineas nodded. "They would."

Phineas reached a house that looked as she'd imagined it, like something out of a fairy tale: low to the ground and covered in vines and weeds. He carried her inside and set her on a bed that was no more than a board covered by a thin blanket. There was only one room, dark and cool, and it smelled smoky. Phineas lit two candles. He busied himself at the corner of the house, opening cabinet doors and then stirring something in a bowl. Mary thought he was making her something to eat, but when he returned, he nodded at her cuts.

In the bowl was paste, and Phineas used a wooden spoon to apply the paste to Mary.

"Use it my own self," Phineas said. "Look at me. As old as old gets."

Mary nodded. She showed him the places it hurt most—below her left ear, her right thigh, both elbows.

As Phineas smeared paste onto each place, Mary thought she could see a pair of eyes peering into the house from a window that wasn't entirely covered with vines.

"It's *him*!" Mary screamed. "It's Andrew come to get me!"

"You're safe with me," Phineas said.

But she wasn't safe with Phineas. She felt in in her chest.

Phineas finished applying paste to Mary's wounds and told her to get some rest.

"I need to go to school," Mary said.

Phineas said, "And who'll be waiting for you there?"

Mary could still see them, Andrew and her old friends, as though they were ghosts now surrounding her, their hands reaching into satchels, pulling out things to throw at her. She understood why her father hung the men he did, those incapable of redemption. She started to drift off as Phineas sat in a chair across the room and lit a pipe, the sweet smoke traveling toward Mary, wrapping around her like a silk cocoon.

Mary was asleep on the old man's bed when a distinct noise invaded her dreams: a hive of bees. The buzzing grew louder and louder, straddling both Mary's dream life and her waking life, and for a moment, as she opened her eyes and tried to focus, she was unsure where she was, whose unfamiliar bed she was in, or what was happening.

The room was lit with four candles now, but it must have been night for she could see flickering torches outside. Mary stumbled out of bed and ran to the window through which she had thought Andrew White was peering earlier. The buzz was a crowd of people outside Phineas' door, some young, some old, including her father, and the door to the shack was about to give way as someone outside attempted to cleave it open with an axe.

Phineas sat calmly in a chair, his eyes fixed on the door.

"What's happening?" Mary asked. Her hands were shaking. Wave after wave of shivers ran up through her.

"They think I've done evil," he said.

Mary, her voice strained, said, "What do you mean?"

Phineas shook his head, resigned. "It's coming to an end now."

Mary approached the door. She yelled, "Go away! Leave us alone!"

"There's no stopping an approaching storm," Phineas said. "I've seen it before."

Each time the axe hit the door, Mary screamed. It was as though the axe was meant for her. And maybe it *was* meant for her—all those things thrown at her earlier that day, pelted as she was by whatever her classmates could get their hands on. Maybe they'd gone to town to gather more people to dole out an even harsher punishment. She remembered his voice, high and shrill: *Behold! The mark of the beast!*

Mary collapsed to the floor as the door split in two. Several people kicked the broken door so that it opened down the middle. Two men pulled her from the old man's house even as she protested, screaming and punching, her heels collecting splinters along the floor.

"What are you *doing*?" she yelled. "Let me *go!*"

That's when she saw a noose hanging from the thick branch of a tree. Sitting in the tree was an older boy she recognized from school, a boy who had once killed a frog with the side of his fist. He had evidently climbed up there to tie the noose to the branch.

Mary was certain they were dragging her to the noose, so certain that she wailed and kicked, tears streaking her face. But then she saw her father lead Phineas T. Rider to the tree, along with two other men, and together they quickly bound his hands behind his back and his ankles together, and then lifted him up into the air so that the older boy in the tree could place the noose around his neck. For a moment, Phineas looked as though he were floating up into the sky on his own, as though God were saving him from the hands of man. But then the boy in the tree tightened the noose around Phineas's neck.

"*No!*" Mary yelled. "He *saved* me!"

"Hush now," an older woman said to Mary. "The devil's speaking through you."

Mary spotted Andrew White in the distance, clutching his Bible in both hands, his lips moving to prayer.

Mary pointed at Andrew White and screamed, "It was *him*. He *attacked me!*"

Andrew White's parents, as fat and pasty as their son, stepped in front of Mary and said, "It's a sin to lie, girl."

"You're murderers!" Mary yelled. "Murderers!"

Because there was no platform for Phineas to stand on, no trapdoor to open beneath his feet, the men let him hang there for a few minutes as he choked, his eyes growing wider.

Finally, Mary's father wrapped his arms around the man's ankles, which dangled near her father's neck, and he yanked down as hard as he could. He did this a few more times, just to be sure that Phineas's neck had indeed snapped.

Fat Andrew White lifted his Bible into the air and said, "For if we live, we live to the Lord, and if we die, we die to the Lord. So then, whether we live or whether we die, we are the Lord's."

"I hate you!" Mary screamed. She broke away from whoever had been holding onto her and charged Andrew. Grabbing his doughy face, she tried sinking her fingers into his eyes. Andrew dropped his Bible and a howl released from his mouth as Mary pressed harder, all the while pushing him backwards, toward a tree. Something had come apart inside her, and she was acutely aware, even as she was doing what she was doing, that her actions were wrong...and yet she couldn't stop. Andrew was helpless—weak, even—and Mary was confident beyond doubt that she could kill the boy.

It took three adults, all men, to pull Mary from Andrew as another man pried her fingers from the boy's eyes. When her fingers came free, she saw that Andrew White's eyes had been clenched shut but that he was crying. She kicked his Bible at him. While a man she didn't know kept his arms wrapped around her torso, her father lifted her legs and held them together to keep her from kicking.

"Get some rope," her father called out.

"You're going to hang me, too, aren't you?" she said. "Good! I want you to!"

"I should," her father said. "But not today. There's still some hope you can be redeemed."

"Is there?" she asked. The words came out of her mouth like venom from a fang.

"There is," his father said calmly. "There surely is."

It was all Mary could do not to spit in his face. She realized that this was her new self, the new Mary, and that whatever line she had crossed would be hard to back away from now. She suddenly hated everyone in this vile town, the adults, her classmates, her own parents. They were all here to make her life miserable, every last one of them, even the babies yet to be born in this unholiest of places. They could all burn in Hell for eternity, as far as she was concerned. Every last one of them.

Part Two

After the incident with Phineas T. Rider—a topic her father refused to discuss—Mary wasn't allowed to return to school. Instead, an old woman named Olivia Purdy, who had been a schoolteacher for over thirty years, came to the house to teach Mary, ending each day with a reading from the Bible, this at the request of Mary's father.

Mary's mother, Bernadette—a tall, striking woman with black hair and eyes as blue as sapphires—often excused herself whenever Mrs. Purdy came over.

"Oh, take the air," Mrs. Purdy liked to say. "It's good for you."

"I think I will," Bernadette would reply, and if Mrs. Purdy wasn't looking, she'd smile and roll her eyes conspiratorially at Mary, an acknowledgment of the old woman's silliness. Mrs. Purdy was, in many ways, silly—she wore tiny glasses on the tip of her nose and enunciated each and every word—but she was also a kind woman who did not think Mary was an evil girl for the things she had done. And Mrs. Purdy would surely have heard about Mary since the entire town had heard. Ten years old, and her fate had been sealed.

Four years came and went—four years during which her father had refused to mention the incident. One day, when Mary was fourteen, Olivia Purdy stopped mid-lesson and said, "I'm not feeling well today, dear. I think we'll just end here."

There were many days that Olivia Purdy didn't feel well—she was never shy about documenting her various aches and pains—but she had never ended a lesson early.

"Are you all right?" Mary asked, reaching down and touching her fang marks, which she did whenever she was nervous, which was often. The fang marks had never gone away. Several times each day, without realizing what she was doing, Mary would reach down and rub two fingers over the marks, the way another person might pinch the bridge of her nose or chew her nails.

"Don't worry about me now," Mrs. Purdy said. "Nothing a little rest won't take care of."

Mary hugged her goodbye and saw her to the door.

"I'll check on you later," Mary said.

Mrs. Purdy nodded then made her way uneasily down the front stoop, heading in the opposite direction from the main thoroughfare. The old woman lived on the outskirts of town in a house no larger than the front room where Mary took her lessons. Mary had been there only twice before, but she could still recall the smallness of the house and the smell of it, like damp dirt and rotting fruit.

After Mrs. Purdy left, Mary paced about, unsure what to do with herself. Then she became worried about Mrs. Purdy. It wasn't like her to leave mid-lesson. What if something serious was wrong with her? She was old, and like a lot of old women Mary had known in her life, Mrs. Purdy was likely to die sooner than later. Mary reached down, about to touch the fang marks again, but caught herself this time. She needed, she realized, to find her mother. Her mother would know what to do.

Outside in the brisk air, Mary couldn't remember the last time she had walked alone while other children were in school, and she worried someone might scold her, grab her by the arm, and take her to her father, whose jail was in a nearby log cabin. She decided it would be best to walk with purpose, head up, long strides, nothing apologetic or meek in her demeanor. Walking past First Hide and Leather National Bank, Peabody's Dry Goods, and the post office, Mary casually glanced around to see if anyone noticed her, but no one gave her a suspicious look. In fact, no one seemed to recognize her. Was it all about how one carried oneself? Was that how one got what one wanted from this world? She continued on, past the feed store and the general store, past the house where Mrs. Kent made dresses while her husband, Mr. Kent, made hats, past the land office. That's when she finally spotted her mother.

Mary hesitated before approaching. Her mother was talking to Ephraim Flynn, the odd fellow who sold medicinal tonics and remedies from a cart he set up each day at the side of the road. What could her mother possibly need from him, this man who sold a bag of live insects to be worn around the neck? Her mother didn't have chicken pox, cholera, or consumption. She didn't suffer from whooping cough or convulsions. Mary wasn't sure what any of these maladies were, but she'd heard people mention them, sometimes whisper them, and she could tell by their expressions that none were good. Did her mother already know about Mrs. Purdy's illness, and was she describing the old woman's symptoms to Ephraim Flynn? But how would she have known this already?

Mary'd had a nightmare once about Ephraim Flynn. In it, Ephraim approached her with his bag of insects and lowered its string over her head, settling it against the back of her neck. As he backed away, the string tightened like a noose, choking Mary, and bugs crawled out from holes in the bag, their tiny legs and antenna touching her flesh. She screamed so loud in the dream that she woke herself up. Covered in sweat and breathing hard, she opened her eyes and swatted her arms and chest, trying to knock away the dozens of bugs that weren't there.

For a moment Mary considered the possibility that her mother was buying a potion for her or her father, but why? Neither was sick. This theory, however, dissolved when Mary saw her mother laughing at something Ephraim had said. When her mother placed the back of her hand against her mouth to hide the laugh, Mary knew with absolute certainty what was happening. She knew because she, too, had laughed that way once.

It had been after church a year ago when Ephraim's son Jeremiah sat next to her on the pew. He had a lazy eye into which Mary could read any number of things, and he had a thick swoop of hair that hung interestingly over his forehead. Throughout the sermon, he had looked over at her several times. One time, he pretended he was falling asleep, but then he opened his eyes wide and smiled at her. After church, as the congregation mingled outside, he walked right up to her and said, "The preacher looks like a toad," and Mary laughed—too loud. And then she raised the back of her hand up to her mouth, to shield her laughter so others wouldn't know. But what she really didn't want anyone to know was that she liked this boy. She liked him in a manner that she had never liked any other boy. Mary thought about him for weeks afterward and imagined all sorts of things she could never tell anyone. Some nights, thinking about him, Mary felt on fire. She'd wake in the middle of the night, tangled in her blankets, her arms wrapped so tightly that she'd be unable to move at first, until, after quite a struggle, she wriggled free.

But Ephraim Flynn? His *father*?

Her mother looked around after she laughed, as Mary would have done, and then she touched Ephraim's shoulder with her fingertips and backed away. Ephraim smiled, but it was furtive, and he quickly packed up his supposed cures into his pushcart. While Mary's mother headed in one direction, Ephraim proceeded in another.

Mary needed to talk to her mother about poor Mrs. Purdy, but she decided to follow Ephraim Flynn instead, although she couldn't have said precisely why. She stayed several yards behind him, surreptitiously glancing behind her, taking ten steps forward before stopping to assess her surroundings. She had to remind herself that the best way to remain invisible was to be visible, and so she held her head up and maintained a confident gait while still calculatedly lagging behind the peculiar man who himself appeared to be on a dire mission.

Ephraim pushed his cart well beyond any of the public businesses, down streets where there were only boarding houses and horses tied to hitching posts. The further he pushed, the fewer boarding houses there were, until he reached a stretch of weedy land on which sat an old barn. There were not many old barns in these parts, since most of the buildings had been constructed in the last ten years when the city officially became a city, but there were, here and there, a few rickety buildings remaining from the first settlers, and this barn appeared to be one of them.

Ephraim pushed his cart into a patch of overgrown shrubs, as though he had done this many times before, and then he walked over to the barn and pulled open one of its large doors. The door creaked shut behind him.

Since no one else was around, Mary decided that now was a good time to be furtive, walking on the balls of her feet, creeping slowly toward the barn. Mary knew this wasn't where he lived because she had been to his house many times, trying to talk Ephraim's son, Jeremiah, into going to the hangings downtown. It was Jeremiah's mother, in fact, who had first spread the notion that Mary was an evil little girl for doing such a thing; it was Jeremiah's mother who mentioned Mary's name in the same breath with Satan's.

Mary crept around the corner of the barn, expecting her mother to appear any second from the direction she and Ephraim had just come. Deep down, she knew this was what would happen, because she knew what sorts of plans she'd have made with Jeremiah if she could have made plans with him. She knew she'd have made such plans because of how her temperature rose at night and because of the kinds of things she thought about, those things that would forever stay inside her head, lest someone use it as proof that she and Satan were indeed of the same mind.

Mary waited.

Sooner or later, she thought. Sooner or later her mother would come walking toward the barn, and all the puzzle's pieces would fit snugly together.

A good deal of time passed before the barn door opened. Mary crouched, expecting to see an impatient Ephraim Flynn, but it was her mother. She must have taken a short cut and arrived before Mary and Ephraim.

Mary's mother brushed off her dress, smoothing the wrinkles, while looking around for spectators, but there were none that she could see. Mary sunk even lower to the ground, but then a sudden fear of a snake biting her caused her to spring back up in plain sight. Fortunately, her mother was already on her way, walking quickly (too quickly, Mary thought) in a part of town where she had no business to be.

Mary made her way promptly to the street, hoping to escape before she was spotted, but when the barn door creaked open again, Ephraim Flynn emerged whistling a tune. Mary froze. He didn't see her right away, as he was busy shutting the barn door and then adjusting his shirt.

While Ephraim walked toward his concealed pushcart, Mary thought she could make a run for it, but then he looked up. A dark look crossed his face at the sight of Mary, as though he wanted to strike her. But then he smiled—a forced smile, Mary thought—and said, "Mary? Is that you?"

"Yes, sir," she said.

"What are you doing all the way out here?"

Mary said, "My teacher is ill. Mrs. Purdy? I was looking for her house to see how she's feeling."

Ephraim said, "Mrs. Purdy lives all the way on the other side of town. Don't you know that?"

"No, sir," Mary lied.

"How long have you been standing there?" Ephraim asked.

"Just long enough to notice your pushcart," Mary said. "I recognized it, and I thought maybe something terrible had happened to you, sir."

"Something *terrible*? Like what?" Ephraim Flynn smiled wider and took several steps toward her. Was he going to murder her?

Mary shrugged. "I don't know. It just didn't seem right. Your cart being there."

"I see," Ephraim said. "And did you notice anything else unusual while you were standing there?"

"No, sir," Mary said.

"Nothing at all?" Ephraim asked.

Mary shook her head. *Be calm*, she told herself. *Be calm.* "How's Jeremiah?" Mary asked.

"Jeremiah?" Ephraim repeated. His smile faded "You're a smart girl, aren't you?"

"I hope he's well," Mary said. "But I really should go find Mrs. Purdy now."

"All right," Ephraim said. "You run along now. You go see how old Mrs. Purdy is doing." Mary took two steps when Ephraim said, "Wait! Here." He pulled his pushcart from the hedges and opened it up. He reached inside and pulled out a blue bottle. He shook it several times and said, "Give this to Mrs. Purdy. It's a tonic. A cure-all. Very effective." Mary reached for the bottle, but Ephraim quickly pulled it back, out of her reach. "But you'd better show this to your mother first. And tell her who gave it to you and where you found me. Tell her you saw me by this old barn and that I gave you this to give to Mrs. Purdy." He wasn't looking anywhere except into her eyes, as if staring at his own reflection inside them. "It's always best to make sure your parents know what you're doing. And that'll keep me from getting into trouble, too." He winked at Mary and then handed over the bottle. Rolling his pushcart away, he called out over his shoulder, "Just make sure she shakes it. Two small sips in the morning. Two small sips at night. And she'll be as good as new! Good day, Mary."

"Good day to you, Mr. Flynn."

Mary didn't give the bottle to her mother or to Mrs. Purdy. She dropped it onto somebody's yard when she didn't think anyone was looking.

By the time she reached her house, her mother was already there, as Mary suspected she would be.

"And where were *you*?" her mother asked, but she wasn't angry, more curious if anything.

"Mrs. Purdy was sick and went home. I thought I'd check on her but didn't know where she lives."

"You do, too, know where she lives," her mother said. "Remember? Over on Webster Street? The last house at the very end of the block?"

Mary shook her head. "I don't feel good myself now."

"You should get some rest," her mother said.

Mary obeyed. In fact, she had wanted to go to bed so that she wouldn't have to face her father, who often said that he could peer into a suspect's eyes and determine what he was hiding. "I see things other men don't," he had said once when Mary had visited him at the jail, his feet up on his desk, ankles crossed. "That's why I'm the Sheriff and not a deputy," he added, staring into her eyes.

No, it was better to steer clear of everyone until she could sift through all the various pieces. Not that nighttime brought any peace. She spent most of it awake thinking, and when she did slip into sleep, she dreamed of Ephraim Flynn and his dreadful bag of live insects. She kept slipping into and out of sleep, but each time it was the same dream—Ephraim placing the bag's string over Mary's head, as though helping her with a gruesome necklace. *Why can't I stop this dream?* she wondered once she had awoken, her chest quickly expanding and contracting. *What's happening to me?*

The next morning, Mrs. Purdy arrived at the usual time. Mary was so happy to see her that she wrapped her arms around Mrs. Purdy and pulled her close. The old woman was short, and since Mary was growing taller by the day, their heights had recently evened out.

"I was worried about you," Mary said, still holding onto Mrs. Purdy.

"Worried about *me*? You shouldn't do that, dear. Why, I survived the cholera epidemic when it swept through and killed an entire town. Not this town. Another town. That was before I moved here, dear. Before you were born. I survived scarlet fever and smallpox, too. You don't go worrying about me now, you hear?" She took Mary by the shoulders and stared at her. "But look at you! You look terrible."

"I couldn't sleep," Mary whispered.

Her mother walked into the room and said, "She came home sick yesterday. Said she went out looking for you." Then, cheerily, she said, "I believe I'll take a morning walk before the weather turns."

"Oh, yes, take the air," Mrs. Purdy said. "It's good for you."

Mary knew her mother was trying to get her attention so that she could roll her eyes, but Mary refused to look. On the one hand, Mary didn't want her mother to leave the house, because leaving the house meant that she would learn from Ephraim Flynn where Mary had been yesterday afternoon. On the other hand, if only to unburden herself of this knowledge, Mary wanted her mother to find out. Both choices, however, made Mary's stomach hurt, and she couldn't help grimacing.

"Oh, dear," Mrs. Purdy said. "Perhaps *you* need the day off today as I did yesterday." In a lowered voice, Mrs. Purdy asked, "Is it your time?"

"My time?" Mary asked, suddenly frightened. Time to *die*? When Mrs. Purdy glanced down in the general direction of Mary's waist, Mary understood what Mrs. Purdy meant.

"When I was your age," Mrs. Purdy said, "they called it 'female hysteria.'" She snorted at the thought.

"Oh," Mary said. Mary really didn't want to talk about this, but no other subject came to her, except for that *other* subject.

"You *do* know what I'm talking about, don't you? You're not a late bloomer, are you?"

"No, I know," Mary said. "It's not that."

"I have some black cohosh, if you want some," Mrs. Purdy said. "It helps my rheumatism."

Mary shook her head. She didn't know what black cohosh was, and she didn't want to know.

"I've been told," Mrs. Purdy said, "that Cannabis Indica is also effective, although I've never personally tried it."

"That's not *it*," Mary said more forcefully than she intended. "That's not the *problem*."

Mrs. Purdy looked as though her feelings were hurt. "Well then," she said gently, opening her satchel, inside of which she kept her daily lessons. "I suppose we should begin."

"I'm sorry," Mary said, but Mrs. Purdy wouldn't look up. "Really," Mary said. "I am."

"I suppose we should talk about your reading assignment," Mrs. Purdy said. "Yes, let's start there."

Mary's mother, stepping through the door a few hours into the day's lessons, looked pale and weak. Even from a distance and with her poor eyesight, Mrs. Purdy remarked on how poorly Mary's mother looked.

"I do believe I've passed something on to Mary and now Mary's passed it on to you," she said. "I suppose the next victim will by the Sheriff."

Mary and her mother looked at each other at the mention of Mary's father. *So*, Mary thought. *You know now.* There was no reversing time. It stood between them, Mary's knowledge of the evil deed. But then the light in the room shifted, as it often did at that time of the day, and Mary saw her mother differently. She saw a sad woman married to a man who never made her laugh, and Mary couldn't help thinking of the tree of knowledge, the way her father had told it from the serpent's perspective.

"I need to lie down, I think," her mother said.

"You do that," Mrs. Purdy said. "Some rest will do you good. It did me good yesterday, that's for sure."

Mary's mother nodded, although her thoughts were clearly across town, where the man with the bottled potions must have stood pining for this sad woman even as he wondered about his own fate. Everything that mattered in life, Mary thought as she watched her mother walk away, hung by the barest of threads.

That night, in her dream, the bugs tore through the canvas sack. In addition to all the ants, grasshoppers, and centipedes, there were wasps, too, and they sunk their stingers into Mary, one after the other, even as their wings brushed against her flesh.

Mary opened her eyes and gasped. There sat her mother on the side of her bed, her fingers gently pinching her, nails digging into her skin. Mary sat up, trying to catch her breath.

"I didn't want to startle you," her mother said.

"It was a dream," said Mary.

"A bad one?"

"It's the bag of bugs," she said, and looked up at her mother for a reaction. Her mother, who held a candle, looked away. This was how it had been earlier during dinner with her father—whenever Mary caught her mother's eye, her mother peered down at her plate.

"Look at me," Mary demanded.

Her mother looked. She'd been crying. Mary could see that now.

"I couldn't sleep last night," Mary said.

Her mother asked, "Are you going to tell him?"

"How do you know I haven't already?" Mary asked.

Her mother said, "We're all still alive."

Mary took a deep breath. She said, "No, I'm not going to tell him. But what about Mr. Flynn? Are you going to keep seeing him?"

"Shhhhhh," her mother said. "You must never mention his name, you hear me?"

"Well?" Mary asked.

Her mother shook her head. "I won't see him again. I promise, love." She said, "He's a good man, though. He knows a lot about the world. He knows where there's a spring that makes a person stay young forever."

"That's Satan talking," Mary said.

"Maybe so," her mother said. "But sometimes you want someone to talk to you. Anyone."

"Even if it's Satan?" Mary asked.

Her mother ignored this last question. Or maybe she was afraid to answer. She put her hand on Mary's cheek. "Good night," she said, then leaned forward and kissed Mary's damp forehead.

Fake News

Jeremy T. Wilson

Faith wanted me to go. She said I could use a break from our daughter Daisy.

"You might learn something," she said.

"About what?"

"About why men turn into clichés."

I already knew the answer. I showed her the video I'd seen on Facebook. It was the other woman. I'd use the word *mistress* if I was the kind of guy who used the word *mistress*. Her name was Sally. She was Tom's receptionist, twenty-eight to his forty-three. In the video she was twerking in front of a mirror while holding a glass of chardonnay.

Faith rolled her eyes. "Fake news," she said.

I didn't want to go fishing with Tom for any number of reasons. I didn't really even like to fish. I didn't want to hear his lame excuses, or worse, be tempted by them. I didn't want to sleep on a boat. I didn't want to have a fish focus its glassy eye on me and beg for its life. But Faith was right. I did need to get away from Daisy.

She'd just finished middle school, and we'd found out recently she'd sent a picture of her boobs to a boy in her class on Snapchat, who then took a screenshot of that picture and circulated it to his squad. I took her phone away and pretty much haven't let her out of the house since, so she's been sulking around like I killed everything she's ever loved, set it all on fire, gathered up the ashes, and made her drink it mixed in a smoothie full of puppy hearts.

Faith thought I was overreacting, and while she certainly didn't condone what Daisy had done, she said I was sending a message to our daughter that she should be ashamed of her body, and that I was making her recognize that her body could be "weaponized." But what Faith was most upset about was that she thought she'd taught Daisy never to seek her own self-worth from the male gaze.

I imagined all these pubescent perverts holding their cell phones under their flies and stroking their peckers while they stared at her pic. I imagined her life, well into the future, sitting at a job interview, her entire online history clickable and scrollable, and there she'd be, lifting her shirt up at some grainy eighth-grade slumber party. And it made me fear for the world Daisy had inherited and had to walk through, a world full of constant voluntary exposure, a world that worships a lack of privacy, pathological frankness, a world afflicted by the curse of having to show *everyone* just how good you are at twerking in front of a mirror.

"They're just my boobs, Dad," she'd said.

This made me furious, because, of course they weren't *just* boobs. The boys didn't ask for pictures of her feet.

I flew to Boston from Chicago and took an Uber out to Salem, where Tom was living the life of an adulterer in a condo all by himself. He waited in the garage next to his Tesla already packed with gear. He wore a white captain's hat outfitted with a gold rope and laurels. I couldn't tell if he was serious about this hat. He was one of those guys who always got into something real heavy and then abandoned it once he got bored. One year for Christmas he sent us all scarves he'd knitted. He made at least a thousand birdhouses in his woodshop. He wrote some bad poetry and collected it all in a self-published chapbook he titled *Seasons*. But a boat was a pretty damn expensive hobby to just toss aside like bad poetry. Or a twenty-year marriage.

On the way to the marina, we stopped at a convenience store and I bought a Styrofoam cooler and loaded it full of beer and ice. Tom didn't drink, but I liked him anyway. Always had. And not just because he was married to one of my wife's best friends. He was funny and warm and generous, and every time we'd spend the weekend or go on vacation together they seemed like a model family. They had two sweet and loving kids who listened to their parents, and they all appeared to get along with one another in that tame, white-bread, colloquial sort of way rich New Englanders have of doing everything.

I wanted to pretend we were all the same people we were last year when we'd planned this trip. I wanted to act like nothing had changed, so I took some Dramamine and relaxed as we cruised out to sea, the wind chapping my cheeks, a cold beer cracked open and sudsy. I was afraid the farther out we went I'd lose service. But did anyone ever lose service anymore? Tom's boat was a Sundancer 350, and according to the manufacturer's website, it could sleep six comfortably in its first-class cabin, *where stylish aesthetics for the jetsetter and power for the explorer combine in perfect harmony*. It wasn't designed to be a fishing boat, but Tom said we could most certainly fish off the swim platform, or at least we were going to try. He kept his eye on some radar-looking device that he claimed was going to drop us on a bunch of fish. It had an orange digital display that projected the undersea terrain, and wherever it promised a mess of fish, a giant orange fish swam into view, like some primitive 8-bit video game.

"I don't even know what kind of fish are out here," he said.

I did some research on my phone. Apparently, striped bass or bluefin tuna were popular in this part of the Atlantic. Striped bass were said to be tricky and unpredictable. I found a good-looking recipe on marthastewart.com. I hoped we wouldn't be the ones to clean them.

"Striped bass," I said. "And bluefin tuna."

"Tuna? Those things are huge."

"You've never done this before?"

"No. I mean, yeah. I've been fishing. On other people's boats, but not my own."

"I guess they just give those captain's hats to anybody."

"Dress for the job you want, not the job you have."

He stopped and dropped anchor, and we cast a couple of rods off the back, which he insisted I correctly call the stern. The rods didn't look as sturdy as I'd imagined they would, like maybe they were ill-suited for the job. I'd pictured the two of us strapped into a chair bolted to the deck, a two-hour fight on the open sea against some monster of the deep. We would finally haul it in, man and fish both exhausted, man triumphant, only to toss the behemoth back to its inky lair, a reminder that we, mankind, are the true and merciful gods. We used shrimp for bait. I told him that didn't seem right, and read to him from the site I still had called up on my phone. "*Live bait such as herring, menhaden, mackerel, eels, squid, clams, anchovies, bloodworms, shad, nightcrawlers, and sandworms all make great bait for striped bass fishing.*"

"Fake news," he said.

We fished for about an hour or more without any luck. I got hungry and took a break while Tom kept fishing with the wrong bait. I drank a beer and ate a ham and cheese sandwich that had been perfectly melted by the warmth of the sun into a soft, almost grilled cheese-like consistency. The only chips Tom had were salt and vinegar, so I passed.

I hadn't heard a peep from anyone else on board, so I was surprised when a girl surfaced from below deck. At first I wondered if I was hallucinating some kind of apparition brought about by our voyage, a siren, a mermaid, a sea maiden, but Tom clearly saw her too, because he went over and kissed her on the lips. Now this was weird to see for a couple of reasons, because for as long as we were all friends I'd never seen him kiss his wife on the lips. But what was even weirder was that she was holding a baby.

"I'm Sally," she said, and held out her hand. I took it and shook, but didn't stand up. "And this is Cody," she said, and bounced the baby in her arms. "We were napping."

I shook the baby's hand with my finger.

Faith had called Sally a "skank." But I took this word with a grain of salt. A woman and her girlfriend scorned and all that. Meeting Sally in person, I wouldn't say there was anything glaringly skanky about her. She wore a striped, hooded pullover, and her brown hair in a ponytail. Her shorts were a respectable length, and, yes, she had nice, tan legs, but nice, tan legs do not make one a skank. She wore white boat shoes. She was catalogue pretty in the way a lot of girls are pretty, the kind of pretty you recognize in the sidebar ad of your email and think for a second that you might click on the ad just to see if there's another picture of her somewhere modeling underwear. But you don't click it.

When my wife told me all about what Tom had done, she never once mentioned that he'd gotten his skanky mistress pregnant and she'd had his kid. So not only was I shocked to find Sally had joined us on our fishing trip, I was also shocked to find a baby on board. The baby wasn't really a baby, at least not an infant. It could walk unsteadily around the boat and toddle toward the nearest trouble. Sally chased him away from the fishing tackle, the dashboard, the stairs, the cooler full of beer. She opened up a compartment under one of the seats and strapped him into a tiny blue-and-white life jacket that he didn't like so much. She gave him some chocolate milk, and he sat down and drank it politely like a little, old man. I could see that he kind of, sort of looked like Tom, but then I did the math, and I wasn't quite sure it could've been Tom's. Unless of course he'd been seeing this woman for a lot longer than any of us had known.

"Did you eat all the sandwiches, babe?" Sally asked.

Tom still had his line in the water hoping for a nibble and must not have heard her, so I handed her the plastic grocery bag where I'd found my sandwich. Sally pulled out two more sandwiches and set them on the table, balled up the plastic bag and stuffed it in the front pocket of her pullover.

"The ocean doesn't need any more trash," she said.

Sally ate her sandwich and drank a Diet Coke. She turned on some music from one of the many dashboard controls. Hall & Oates. She was not even alive when Hall & Oates was putting that kiss on their list of the best things in life. I looked it up. 1980.

"Why aren't you fishing?" she asked.

"Inferior bait."

She looked at Tom with his line out there in the dark water, then scooted next to where I was sitting. She leaned in close and whispered in my ear. "Tom doesn't know what he's doing."

I laughed. "The captain's hat is just a ruse."

"Do you know what you're doing?"

"Woah!" Tom shouted. His rod was arched like an eyebrow. He'd hooked a big one and was turning pink he was straining so hard to work the reel. I thought the whole thing was going to snap. The rod. The line. Tom.

Sally nudged me with her elbow. "Help him."

I didn't want to interfere with another man's catch, even if he was struggling, but I did want to get a closer look, so I went out there and stood behind him on the swim platform.

"I got this," he said, and grit his teeth.

Cody peeked over the backseat and threw his chocolate milk box into the ocean. Sally put him in her lap and we all watched Tom's impression of a competent sport fisherman.

"What do you think it is?" I asked.

"Moby Dick," Tom said.

Just then the line snapped and Tom fell backwards into me, knocking us both off our feet, the two of us careening onto the platform, scrambling not to fall into the water, a pair of seadog buffoons. We lay there looking up at Sally and Cody, who both shared the same look on their faces, the same pretty faces. And that look was pity.

That night we had dinner under a star-speckled sky, more stars than I'd probably ever seen in my life. Sally spread out a pink gingham tablecloth and served us all a feast of cured meats, olives, pate, brie, and a baguette. We all cozied up under heavy wool blankets because when the sun went down the sea chilled our bones. Sally had brought some wine, too, a rosé that even Tom felt compelled to sip. Times were changing. Cody was already asleep in the cabin, gently being swayed into his dreams. Sally said he always slept so good on the boat.

"What if it was a giant squid?" she asked. "I just read an awesome book about giant squid."

"People still read books?" I asked.

She picked up her phone. It was held inside a rubbery case designed with the old-school New England Patriots logo. "I have like 200 books in here."

"Those aren't books," I said.

"Whatever, if we get lost at sea I won't run out of stuff to read. What'd you bring?"

It was obvious she wanted me to say "beer" and to realize how worthless my cargo was compared to her digital library, but I didn't bite.

"You don't catch giant squid out here," Tom said.

"*You* don't catch anything," Sally said. "So how do you know it wasn't a giant squid?"

She showed us all a picture of a giant squid on her phone. I was glad the line had snapped. "By your logic it could've been an Oldsmobile," Tom said.

"Sure! Why limit the potential of the unknown?"

"Because there are certain limits," Tom said. He tossed off the blanket and went downstairs to the head, which is what he kept insisting I call the bathroom.

Sally swiped her thumb across her phone and held it up to the sky. The pattern of the stars beamed on the screen, like she was holding an empty frame that we could see clear through to the heavens.

"Ursa major," she said, and moved closer to me. She waved the magic screen around the sky where it named everything we were looking at, like a god. Ursa minor. Cepheus. Leo. She smelled like saltwater taffy.

I downloaded the app so I could be my own god.

"Tom's a romantic," she said. "But his wife had him doomed to realism. I help him be what he's always wanted to be."

I pointed my phone at the sky. The screen told me I was looking at Venus.

"I can tell you really care about people," she said. "You're a good friend. He thought you wouldn't come. But it means a lot to him."

The toilet flushed, or rather didn't flush, but sucked itself into some place well within the boat, where our piss and shit were stored until we could get somewhere to have it all pumped out.

My wife texted: catch anything?

I texted back a squid emoji.

The first-class cabin was as comfortable as the internet promised, so I was pleased to get a good night sleep behind my privacy curtain. In the morning, Tom and I had instant coffee out on the deck while Sally stayed below feeding the baby. The whole world was crystalized and shimmering. The sun crested off the waves in bright diamonds that would've burned my eyes if Tom hadn't let me borrow some expensive sunglasses he'd bought at Nordstrom.

He told me how much he loved the baby, how this baby had renewed him, rejuvenated him in a way his spoiled teenagers could not. He said he wanted to keep little Cody that small forever, "wide-eyed with terror and wonder." Those were his words. I couldn't remember the last time I'd ever felt that way.

"You think I'm a bad guy. Don't you?" Tom asked.

I had thought about the right way to answer this question. If my wife asked me, I'd have to say yes, he was an awful, terrible guy, a total douchebag. But I understood where he was coming from. You live a life with a woman for twenty years. You and your spouse start to realize you really have nothing in common anymore other than the kids. You haven't had sex in months. And a girl comes along to pay a new kind of attention to you, an attention you haven't gotten in a long, long time, shows you a side of yourself you thought was missing or never knew was there. "I'm sure you understand why some people might think so," I said.

"Like Faith."

"And others."

"When I went to the grocery store, she used to call and tell me where to find the milk. Don't you think I could find it myself?"

"What a terrible person."

"Hey, I know I've broken something we all thought would never break, all right, but everything breaks. And it can feel good to break things. You know why? Because it hits you right in the gut. It makes you shiver. Your heart race. You feel that heart pumping inside your chest, and you know you're alive for just a blip. We live under the illusion of permanence, man."

Tom had never talked like this before. Tom had never uttered one word to me about his feelings. Tom was the kind of person who refused to dance when everyone else was dancing. Sally had either brought forth something that had long been tamped down or was feeding him lines of bullshit to justify his sins.

"I really am sorry," he said. "I accept the blame here. But one day they're all going to thank me for waking them the hell up."

Tom clearly wanted me to be his messenger. This was why Sally and the baby were on the trip. I was supposed to like her, which I did. We'd bonded under the stars. And I was supposed to go home and tell my wife that Sally had come along with us and she was a peach. And I was supposed to tell her that Tom felt bad for everything he'd done, but was really a romantic, and that he knew he'd broken something, but that was part of the thrill. He'd actually done them all a favor. The kids. His wife. Himself. He'd made them all realize that nothing is permanent, and because nothing is permanent, we should take nothing for granted. This was what he'd learned, and it had allowed him to live his life in a way he had not been able to before. Oh, and another thing, he's got a baby.

I Googled the phrases *illusion of permanence* and *wide-eyed with terror and wonder*. I found a TED talk from a dude who designed self-driving cars.

I asked Tom if the baby was his.

"It's not not my baby," he said.

I didn't feel like fishing, so I let Sally use my rod. I drank the beer I'd brought and kept an eye on Cody so he wouldn't fall overboard. If he did, could things go back to the way they were before? It was a terrible thought, but one I had nonetheless. The kid had on his blue-and-white life jacket anyway.

I didn't know Sally'd caught anything, until she lifted up the tip of the rod and I saw what was dangling from it, not thrashing or freaking out like most fish out of water, but calmly succumbing to its lot, like, *yeah, you got me, I was so stupid and greedy to go after that piece of shrimp, oh, well, bon appétit!*

Cody toddled after the fish.

"Don't touch!" Tom said, and scooped up the baby in his arms. "It could be poisonous." Something about that hat he was wearing made this all believable.

"What is it?" Sally asked.

The fish was long and thin, about the size and shape of a machete blade, and the sun bounced off its scales in rainbows. It had an unheard of number of fins, like it had sprouted extras as a status symbol, and the fin on top of its spine, whatever that one's called, was sharp and saw-toothed. Its gills widened as it suffocated, and I could see inside its body something purple and vital, losing its color. It had giant eyes that locked in on me, almost like a person's eyes. Not the usual dead eyes of sea life. They were green and pleading.

"Toss it back," I said.

Tom held Cody in one arm and took a picture of Sally and her catch with his free hand. "Put it in your cooler," Tom said, and raced down the stairs with Cody.

"I've still got some beer."

Sally let the rod fall to the deck and the fish did one flop as if it was turning itself on the grill, which the Sundancer 350 came equipped with. The lid squeaked when she took the top off my cooler. She pulled out the cans of beer in a hurry.

"This is a freaking yacht," I reminded her. "Isn't there some well or something where you're supposed to keep fish?"

"You can put your beer in the fridge," she said.

Tom came back with a steak knife and an empty Costco-sized carton of animal crackers. Cody shrieked from the cabin. Tom handed me the empty carton and told me to fill it with seawater, then he lifted up the fishing line, held the fish above the cooler, and cut the line with the steak knife so the fish dropped right in with a squeak and a thud. By now I could smell the fish, something metallic and fearful, like a car accident. I went to the stern and scooped up some water in the animal cracker carton and poured the water in the cooler. I swear the fish smiled at me. I got some more water and filled up the cooler, until all those fins were working and its gills were sucking in its sustenance. This was one crazy-looking fish. I took a picture. It was still looking at me, all curled up in its tight quarters. It had a long, thin snout, and maybe some teeth, and maybe a brood of caviar in the sea, waiting to blossom into a family of thin-snouted, green-eyed fish full of extravagant fins. They were probably all missing this guy. For some reason it looked like it should be wearing glasses. I used the picture I took to search for the fish on my phone. I got a lot of different results and showed them all to Tom. We both agreed. None of them were quite like this fish. I searched for *Atlantic fish full of fins* and got a bunch of pictures of tuna and an article about how fins evolved into feet. I searched *Fish wearing glasses*. Mr. Limpet and that Star-Kist guy.

"Doesn't exist," Tom said. "We've discovered a new species."

Sally picked up her own phone, kneeled beside the cooler, and snapped pictures of the fish, being sure to include herself, posed with a peace sign, in almost every shot.

Later that afternoon, when the beer was all gone and we were getting ready to head home, I took the lid off the cooler and poured the fish back in the ocean.

When they saw the empty cooler, I tried to claim it was a miracle, that the fish could fly, or had evolved quickly, sprouted feet from one of its many fins and leapt right on back to the sea where it belonged.

"You're drunk," Tom said.

"You're a douchebag," I said.

Sally scrolled through her phone. "Somebody on Insta says it's a prasinamata. It's prehistoric. Thought to be extinct."

Tom looked at me like he wanted to toss me overboard with the fish.

Just what the hell did he think he was doing out here anyway?

"Fake news," I said.

When I got home I didn't say anything to Faith about the baby or the supposed dinosaur Sally had lifted from extinction. I knew I was going to have to say something eventually, because she'd find out eventually— if she didn't already know—but I was tired and didn't want to deal with it all right away.

"How's Tom?" she asked.

"He's a romantic now," I said.

"Give me a fucking break," she said.

That night my daughter and I watched an episode of *Seinfeld*. This was something we did a lot, watch old shows together. Daisy preferred *Friends*, so most of the time we'd watch at least one episode of each. We hadn't spoken much since I took her phone away and lectured her about the picture and about life online and about how nothing disappears anymore and how everything we're doing, everything *she's* doing, is being collected, and there is no erasing history anymore, which makes it ever more difficult to make mistakes, or ask for forgiveness.

The episode was the one with the bubble boy, where everyone gets split up on the way to Susan's family cabin, and Kramer gets there first and accidentally burns it down. I read an article on the internet that talked about how every *Seinfeld* plot would've never been possible if they'd had smartphones. You know the one where they wander around the parking garage? Somebody's phone would've remembered where the car was parked. When Jerry forgot the name of his girlfriend but knew it rhymed with a female body part, Not-Mulva, he could've Googled her, looked her up on Facebook or LinkedIn. He probably would've met her on Tinder. The odds were that if they'd had phones there would've been a record somewhere of their meeting, some digital trail between the two of them. Just like the digital trail Daisy streaked across the screens of all her middle school classmates.

"If they had smartphones nobody would've been lost," I said.

"I was just thinking the same thing," Daisy said.

I took out my phone and showed her the app. The one with the stars.

"I've seen that," she said.

"Let's give it a try."

"Too much light pollution."

"Stop being so negative."

I paused the episode and we went outside in the backyard. I held my phone up to the sky, and the screen told me all the stars that were supposed to be there, but in the city they weren't there. Daisy was right. Too much light pollution.

"When do I get my phone back?" she asked.

I didn't have an exact answer for that. Faith and I hadn't discussed it.

"Tom and his receptionist have a baby."

"No way!"

"Yeah."

"Did you tell Mom?"

"Not yet. She may already know. I don't know."

"That's so messed up."

I showed her the picture of the fish in the cooler. "That's her."

She laughed, a sound I didn't know I'd been missing. "Dad?"

"Yeah?"

"Please don't fuck your receptionist."

I'd never heard her say that word before. It felt so childish coming out of her mouth, like she was playing the role of an adult only by adopting our vulgarity. And maybe that's not such a bad thing. Let the kids try all our bullshit out for themselves while it's still safe, before anybody can get too hurt, while they all have so much life left to heal. I didn't have a receptionist, but that was beside the point.

I put my phone away. "Out in the ocean I could see Venus."

"Are we seriously outside looking at stars right now?"

"Venus is a planet."

"I know that you're really trying real hard to have a moment here. Looking at stars. Telling me secrets and all."

"I won't fuck my receptionist."

"So can I have my phone back?" She gave me a giant, pleading fake smile.

I nodded. "It's in the—"

"I know where it is."

She shut the door behind her and went upstairs to her room. I stayed out in the yard looking for stars. The only lights I could make out were from the planes taking off and landing at O'Hare. I wished there was an app I could hold to the sky that would tell me where they'd all come from, or where they might be going.

The World Is on Fire So You Have to Protect Yourself

Betsy Finesilver Haberl

The world is on fire so you have to protect yourself. The good news is that there are easy ways to do so.

First, be a man. You're more likely to avoid the flames that way.

If you're not a man, the next step is to always be alone. Other people spread the fire.

The best way to avoid people is to never leave your house.

Stay inside and look out your window. You see a woman going past on the sidewalk. She is moving quickly, like she wants to run while still appearing as if she's walking. It's snowing, even though it's sunny and only October. She leaves a trail of red, hot embers instead of footsteps in the snow. She keeps glancing over her shoulder.

Behind her, a man follows, walking casually. His hands are in his pockets. He kicks her embers out of the way as he walks, hardly even noticing that he's doing so.

Turn away from the window and don't think about why she's on fire. Women who think about the fire end up feeling a slow burn in the pit of their stomachs. It never ends, and over time the heat seeps into their bones and turns their skeletons to charcoal. They ache whenever they move.

Don't watch the news. Don't read the news. Avoid social media. Otherwise, here's what will happen:

You'll see a video of a middle-aged woman with glasses pushing blonde hair out of her face. She's in a Senate hearing room. She's facing a row of men and telling them about being held down on a bed when she was a teenager. She doesn't remember the where or the when, exactly, but she knows she knows she knows what happened. You can see her heart beating inside of her chest and your heart beats at the same time. You look at her face and you know that since that day she has felt the fire inside of her, in the back of her eye sockets and underneath her fingernails, in places she never thought she could even feel heat.

Behind the men in the room, the wall is covered with heavy wood. You wonder how it's possible that the wood hasn't burst into open flames, that the room is still there, nothing has turned to ash. But remember: they are men. They are there to protect that space, that wooden wall. Their bodies are like cold water, a barrier for the fire.

Turn off the television or put your computer to sleep or shove your phone inside your pocket or close the newspaper and recycle it.

Better yet, throw everything away.

Lock your doors and breathe a sigh of relief when you see they are already locked.

Your daughter is taking a nap. She is just a little girl. Make yourself a cup of coffee and peek in at her. Sit on the floor in the dimly lit room and breathe in the same air that she's breathing.

But it's too late. Your hands, which are wrapped tightly around your coffee mug, are starting to glow from the heat inside your fingertips. Tell yourself it's just warmth from the hot coffee. But you know that's not true at all, that it's been in your blood for a long time.

You have your own story. It's not all that different from the story you just heard on the news.

Tell yourself it's not all that different. Tell yourself everyone has a story like that, the woman on the sidewalk, the woman on the TV, your mother, your first-grade teacher, the actress from that show you watched in high school. Tell yourself it's just something that happened a long time ago. Tell yourself all the ways that you don't even think about it anymore.

Your daughter wakes up from her nap. Pick her up and don't worry about burning her. Only you can feel the heat in your hands. She likes to snuggle on your shoulder as she settles into wakefulness. She's so warm and calm. Carry her to the kitchen and open the fridge. Pour her a glass of milk and realize you can remember his first name, but not his last.

Give your daughter a cup of Goldfish crackers. Slice an apple for her. Listen to the satisfying crunch of the knife cutting through the fruit and remember it was April 25, at a friend's apartment, and you were twenty years old.

Watch your daughter become enchanted by the snowflakes collecting in the grass. She presses the palms of her hands to the window and asks to go outside.

Since you're already on fire, you might as well leave the house. Your daughter is just a child. It's not fair to keep her away from the world just because it's on fire.

Outside, the snowflakes are soft and thick. They swirl around your daughter's feet with each gust of wind, and you remember that you felt frozen, on April 25, but you cannot remember if you said no, or nothing, or moved at all.

Your cheeks and ears feel flushed and hot and you wonder if someone is watching the two of you. Take off your jacket and put your daughter in the stroller.

If you decide to leave your house, it's best to always be moving.

You pass a church with a small playground. It's empty. Your daughter asks to play but you say no, not today. You push her stroller and the wind spins the rusty merry-go-round. Even when you are past the park, you can hear the metallic scrape of the merry-go-round as it spins and spins and spins.

Your daughter asks if she can walk and you say yes. She likes stamping her feet in the light dusting of snow. She runs a little ways ahead of you. Remind her not to go too far away. The sidewalk stretches ahead seemingly forever and you start listing all the things you could have done differently that night to avoid being on fire: not been a woman, not left the house, not left the house at night, not left the house alone, not had friends, not flirted, not been frozen still and quiet when you should have yelled and kicked and screamed.

But remember: the whole damn world is on fire. It's not just you.

The sun is starting to set and the sky glows orange and yellow through the gray clouds. Your daughter is silhouetted darkly against the light and you realize, with horror, that the flames are already dancing around her toes. The colors are the same as the sunset.

But watch what she does. She skips right through them.

You jog a few steps to catch up with her. She stops and throws her head back, opens her mouth to catch snowflakes on her tongue. You look up at the sky with her. The wind is cold on your face like a slap, but you refuse to close your eyes. You imagine what the sky looks like on the other side of the dense clouds. It must be cool and clear as it bends toward the distant horizon.

Keep thinking about that horizon, how the sky curves to meet it, how the setting sun dips below it every day without fail. If you think about the horizon, you won't think about your daughter being a woman in this place, and how for a woman in this place, the world is on fire and there is no way to protect yourself.

St. Crispin's Day

Giano Cromley

One night, every year, Mom and Dad went out, along with all the other moms and dads in the neighborhood. We had no idea what they did, but they didn't come back until late. Sometimes it was light out by the time they got home. They always wore masks. Masks were part of it too.

Mom and Dad always took a long time to get ready. They were playful in the bathroom, listening to music on the tiny red speaker. Mom put on makeup. Dad shaved and splashed on cologne. The smells coming from the bathroom felt new to us and made Mom and Dad seem like different people.

This year, they wore dog masks. Dad's was a German shepherd. He pulled it over his head and looked at himself in the mirror and made a *woof-woof-grrr* sound. It looked strange with his jacket and tie. Mom's poodle mask was lying on the floor next to the sink.

"Why are you going out tonight?" we asked.

"It's St. Crispin's Day," Mom said as she drew makeup under her eye. "We do this every year."

"Who's St. Crispin?" we asked.

"He's very old," Dad said. "So old no one remembers why they even remember him."

Mom and Dad had gone out every St. Crispin's Day for as long as we'd lived in this neighborhood. And we'd lived there as long as any of us could remember, even Terrance.

We liked our neighborhood, mostly because there were lots of kids our age. We played great games of Spud, six different kinds of Tag, Sardines, Kick the Can, Bloody Murder, you name it. Usually we played in the front yard. Sometimes in the backyard, in the shadows of the woods that surrounded us.

It wasn't all great, though. There were teenagers that drove too fast up and down the streets. They'd park and sit on the hoods of their cars. Sometimes they'd knock over garbage cans or bash mailboxes with baseball bats. Mom was always complaining about the teenagers. She called them a "bad element."

"Did you see that one in the pickup?" she'd say to Dad. "With that flag in the back window? I don't think he even lives around here."

"We were teenagers driving too fast once," he'd say. "Our kids'll be teenagers driving too fast one day. Circle of life." By the time he was done talking, he'd have a little smile on his face.

We could tell Mom hated it when Dad smiled like that. Under her breath, she'd whisper, *Thanks so much for listening.*

"Who's babysitting tonight?" For us, this was the most important question.

"Marisol," Mom said.

"Yay!" we shouted.

Marisol was nice, and she was pretty, and she did something with the popcorn that made it taste delicious. We all liked Marisol, but Terrance liked her a little bit more. Terrance used to be called Pink Terrance, but now that he was older, he wanted everyone to call him just Terrance, which we mostly did.

Marisol was getting older too. She didn't babysit as often as she used to. One day, when we were playing Sprinkler Tag in the front yard, a teenager was driving too fast by the house, and we could swear we saw Marisol riding in the passenger seat. But we didn't tell Mom, since we worried she wouldn't let her babysit for us anymore.

"I don't think it's fair, you guys get to go out and we have to stay at home." Little Judy buried her face in a pillow. She was always making declarations. Usually she said the things we wanted to say but were too afraid to. She was the youngest; she didn't know any better.

"There's a lot of things in the world that aren't fair," Mom said. "Try being a grown adult, with a house full of kids always screaming in your ear, and not ever getting a minute to yourself."

Dad joined in, "Or paying the bills, and working every day even when you don't want to."

"*Then* we can talk about what's fair," Mom added.

Little Judy shook her head and bit the pillow. Dad gargled mouthwash. Mom slipped on high heels. The doorbell rang.

We piled out of their bed and raced downstairs. Marisol had on a blue flannel shirt and a pair of jeans with a tear in them. We could see the skin of her knee through the tear. She had a backpack hanging off her left shoulder. Her hair was black and curly, and tonight she wore it pulled back in a poofy ponytail.

"Thank you so much for coming over," Mom said, shooing us away from the door. "It's getting harder and harder to find someone to sit for St. Crispin's."

"It's not a problem." Marisol set her backpack near the door.

"Pizza's already ordered and paid for," Mom said. "Should be here in an hour. Kids in bed by nine. And this one," she pointed at Little Judy, "has been told not to give you any grief tonight."

"Aww, she never gives me grief." Marisol ruffled Little Judy's hair. "Besides, if they want some *real* fun, they can help me study for AP Bio. How's that sound, kids?"

"Booo!" we all shouted.

"Let's make popcorn!" Little Judy said.

"Okay," Mom said, "looks like everything is all together."

Dad came downstairs wearing his German shepherd mask. He couldn't see too well, and he stumbled on the landing. Mom put on her poodle mask. The two of them stood next to each other, posing, even though no one was taking their picture.

"You know the number if anything comes up," Mom said.

Marisol gave her an okay sign.

"But let's make sure nothing comes up." Dad was giggling.

"We're at the Norwoods' this year," Mom said. "You know which one their place is?"

"I passed it on my way here," Marisol said.

"Let's take our leave, m'lady." Dad put his arm out, and Mom took it. "St. Crispin awaits."

They walked out the door, and began cutting across the lawn. The Norwoods' house was four blocks away. Mom and Dad waved. We stood on the porch watching our parents—both wearing dog masks—march over the grass in the fading light.

"I want to watch *Kid Copz*," Slow Winston said. "We always get to watch *Kid Copz*."

"Noooo," Little Judy said. "*Kid Copz* sucks."

"Does your mom know you use that word?" Marisol looked at Little Judy.

"She knows, but she doesn't like it," Slow Winston said.

We noticed Terrance had disappeared, but we didn't care enough to make a big deal out of it. He'd been spending more time alone in his bedroom lately. We'd decided Terrance was turning weird.

Slow Winston turned on the TV. In tonight's episode, Pinkie Cop was trying to catch Cat Burglar robbing the Fish Factory. Sergeant

Ellroy said if Pinkie Cop couldn't stop the heist, then maybe she wasn't meant to be a kid cop. Slow Winston, as usual, sat on the floor, close to the TV. He said this was on account of his cross-eyes. The rest of us gathered around Marisol on the couch.

It was almost dark out. The sliding door to the backyard was showing our reflection back to us, but we could just make out the outlines of the swing set. Marisol was braiding Little Judy's hair.

"What do moms and dads do on St. Crispin's Day?" we asked.

"I don't know," she said. "I'm not a mom or dad." She was watching *Kid Copz*, but she wasn't really watching it.

"You're older than us," we said. "You're closer to being a mom or dad than we are."

She smiled when we said this. Marisol was easily the prettiest babysitter we'd ever had, with big brown eyes and freckles on her cheeks. "The moms and dads around here have one night where they get to have fun," she said.

"Watching *Kid Copz* is fun," Slow Winston said from the floor. He only said it because there was a commercial on.

"Sometimes moms and dads want a different kind of fun."

We didn't know what Marisol meant by this, only that it made us feel left out.

On *Kid Copz*, Pinkie Cop was making a deal with Cat Burglar about not robbing the Fish Factory. To seal the deal, they both spit on their hands before shaking.

"What a terrible show," Little Judy said. "Just terrible."

"Hey, where's Terrance?" Marisol asked.

"He's in his room," we told her. "He's always in his room."

"Terrance!" Marisol could have a loud voice when she wanted to. "Are you okay up there, Terrance?"

Just then, Little Judy leapt up from the couch. She did it so fast that Marisol barely had a chance to let go of the braid she was making.

"What was that?" Little Judy shouted.

"What was what?" we asked.

Little Judy pointed at the sliding glass door. "Out there! In the woods!"

"What did you see?" we asked.

"A man in white!"

Our eyes followed Little Judy's finger. The porch light was on, but it barely cast a glow over the deck. The rest of the backyard was dark. And the woods at the edge of the yard were black.

"Tell me exactly what you saw." Marisol sounded calm, which made us feel better.

"I was looking out there and saw this blur in the woods, so I kept looking and then this guy, maybe a teenager, but dressed all in white, stepped out of the woods and was looking this way. And then he stepped backwards into the woods and disappeared."

We all looked, but we couldn't see a man in white anywhere.

"That's what I saw," Little Judy said.

Terrance came into the living room. "Did someone call me?" His hair was messed up like he'd been asleep.

"Little Judy saw someone in the woods!" we told him.

"Probably a jogger," he said. "There's jogging trails all over the place back there."

"But he was wearing all white," we insisted.

"Let's not get carried away," Marisol said. "We don't know enough to get carried away."

"It was a teenager," Little Judy declared. "I know it was."

Then the doorbell rang.

We all screamed and huddled on the couch. We could tell Marisol wanted to huddle with us, but she was trying to be an adult. Adults can't just scream and huddle on the couch the first time the doorbell rings. She got up.

"Don't answer it!" we shouted. "It could be the man in white! Let's hide!"

But she didn't listen to us. She walked out of the living room and down the hallway.

"Should we pray?" Slow Winston asked.

"Praying won't help," Terrance said.

Some of us were listening to the sounds in the hallway. Some of us were scanning the trees along the edge of the backyard. We weren't sure what we should be more afraid of.

"She just opened the door." Little Judy was listening to Marisol. "I hear voices. Oh god!"

We all scrambled for the couch again. We were climbing over each other, elbows poking eye sockets, knees mashing kidneys, fingernails catching skin.

Then—*whoosh*—Marisol sprang into the living room and shouted: "Pizza's here!"

We screamed. We scrambled some more. Slow Winston fell off the side of the couch and landed on his butt. Then we laughed at how silly the whole thing was. Even Slow Winston laughed as he rubbed his big butt. We'd let our imagination run away from us. Maybe we'd seen too many scary movies. Marisol was here, and she'd always protect us, and pizza was here, and everything seemed better with pizza.

Marisol let us eat in the living room on the condition that we wouldn't tell Mom and Dad. Also on the condition that we wouldn't watch any more *Kid Copz*. Everyone agreed, except Slow Winston, but he was outnumbered.

"How about this one?" Marisol said, switching the channels. "It's called *Fashion Police*."

We'd never heard of *Fashion Police*, and we weren't even sure if we were allowed to watch it.

"It's where they drive around until they find someone who's dressing badly, and then they kidnap them and take them back to their studio and give them a makeover."

"It sounds scary," Slow Winston said.

"It's funny," Marisol said, "because the people dress so badly, and then it's nice because they get to keep the new clothes once they get the makeover."

"That sounds good," Terrance said. "It's a show for grownups."

The rest of us didn't feel like arguing. At least we had pizza, and at least we got to eat it in the living room. Things could be a lot worse.

On the TV, a fat man was walking down the sidewalk and the Fashion Police pulled up alongside him and shouted at him through a megaphone.

Marisol's phone made a ding. She looked at it, then started typing.

"Whatcha typing?" Little Judy asked.

"I'm texting."

"Whatcha texting?"

"A friend of mine is watching *Fashion Police* too. He thinks it's hilarious."

"*He*?" Little Judy was perceptive.

"Yes, he."

"It's a *boy*? Who's a *friend*?"

"Yes."

"So . . . a boyfriend? You have a *boyfriend*?"

Everything went quiet. Terrance was blushing, which is part of the reason we used to call him Pink Terrance. The Fashion Police were hustling to give the fat guy his final makeover.

"I want popcorn," Slow Winston said.

"Yay popcorn!" we shouted. "Make it the way you make it," we told Marisol.

She hit pause on the TV and got up and went into the kitchen. The screen was frozen on the fat guy's face. He was wearing makeup to hide his pimples. Underneath, we could tell he was scared.

"*Kid Copz* is better than *Fashion Police*," Slow Winston whispered to us.

"Yes, it is," Little Judy said quietly. "Yes, it sure is."

"I think this is okay," Terrance said.

"Marisol's already got a boyfriend," we told him. "You're too late."

Terrance blushed some more and sighed loudly.

No one could remember who saw it first, because it started off small and slowly grew. It was a light, in the backyard.

"Does anyone else see that?" Slow Winston asked.

"Yes," we all said.

By now it was the size of a campfire. It was right in front of the swing set because we could see the light reflecting off the monkey bars and curly slide. Everything else in the backyard was pitch black. Maybe because it came on so slowly, none of us shouted or screamed. We just watched the flames flicker and leap and grow.

Marisol was still in the kitchen. We could hear the popcorn popping.

"Pretty quiet in there," she called out to us. "You haven't murdered each other, have you?"

We didn't say anything.

There was movement. Something came out of the darkness and stood by the fire. It was the man in white. It looked like he was wearing a sheet with a hood on it, kind of like a ghost. He walked out of the woods and stood by the fire.

It was quiet for a long time. We didn't know what to do or what he wanted. Then, out of the darkness, another man in white appeared. This one walked weird, as if he didn't have to take steps to move. He stood next to the other man in white at the fire.

Then a third man in white appeared. He moved quicker than the second man in white. Then a fourth and a fifth came out at the same time. They made a circle around the fire.

"I'm putting the special seasoning on the popcorn." Marisol was still in the kitchen.

"Maybe they're ghosts," Slow Winston said.

No one else said anything. Even Little Judy was speechless.

A minute passed. The men in white didn't move. We couldn't see their faces, couldn't see their eyes, or even if they had eyes.

"Okay, you little church mice, here it is."

Marisol came out from the kitchen carrying the big metal bowl that we only ever used on movie nights because it held so much popcorn. She came into the room and stopped. What she first saw was us, not looking at the TV, but instead looking out the sliding glass door. Then she followed our stares out to the back, and that's when she saw what we saw.

"Terrance, hand me my phone." Her voice sounded strange. It was calm, but too calm. "Terrance, where's my phone?"

He didn't move. His mouth was opening and closing like he might be trying to talk.

Marisol put the popcorn bowl on the coffee table, but she set it too close to the edge. It tipped and went over, and as it went, it threw a shower of hot popcorn in the air, and it landed all over us and the couch and the floor, and that was what finally broke the spell.

Little Judy screamed, and Slow Winston joined in, and then everyone, including Marisol and Terrance, started screaming and huddling on the couch.

Finally, Marisol managed to catch herself. She got up and went to the door, and pulled the curtains closed. Now that we couldn't see the men in white, the rest of us got quiet.

"Little Judy, you're sitting on my phone."

Marisol reached under her and pulled out the phone. We could see her hands were shaking, and that made us even more nervous. She pulled up Mom's number.

It rang and went straight to voicemail.

"Fuck!" Marisol said.

"Hey," Slow Winston started to say, but then decided not to make a fuss about swears.

She tried Mom's number again. Then again. Finally, she left a voicemail.

"Mrs. Garvey, this is Marisol. There's something going on here at the house. Something . . . I don't know. There's strange men. I need you to call me back. Please? Okay."

She hung up and looked at us. Then she went to the window and pulled the curtain to the side so she could peek out.

"Fuck!"

None of us bothered to say anything about swears this time.

"Okay," she said. "I'm sure this is okay. It's nothing. Probably. Probably a prank. A messed-up prank on St. Crispin's Day."

She looked out the window again. The firelight from outside caught her face.

"What if it's ghosts?" Slow Winston said.

Marisol pressed *9-1-1* and *send.*

"Hello—yes—there are strange men—in the backyard—I don't know—wearing costumes—I don't know—3355 Cripple Creek Lane—yes—Marisol—I'm the babysitter—Garvey—I don't know—sir, I don't know—white, it looks like robes—I don't know—no—I'm not—sir, I'm not—this isn't a—yes, sir, I know what day it is—this isn't—please—sir, please, listen—I'm sorry—I didn't mean to raise my voice—I'm trying to—I don't know—I don't—why won't you—please—sir—please—"

She pulled the phone from her ear, and we could see they'd hung up on her. It was quiet for a long time. Marisol's face looked different, like she'd just realized something important about how the world works.

"What did they say?" Slow Winston asked.

"They think it's a prank," she said. "They have more important things to do."

"Maybe the men in white are gone," Little Judy said. "Maybe they had their fun and now that they think the cops are coming maybe they left."

We all went to a corner of the curtain and pulled it back to look. It was the same five men standing around the fire in the backyard. It didn't seem like they'd moved a single muscle since the last time we'd looked. There was something about the way they stood, feet set shoulder-width apart, arms crossed, they looked like they belonged there, like we were the ones invading their property.

"What do they want?" Terrance asked.

"This is ridiculous," Marisol said. "Someone needs to find out." She sat us all down on the couch. "Listen," she said, "I'm just going to talk to them. It's no big deal."

"No, no, no!" we all shouted. "Don't go!"

"They're trying to scare us, so I'm going out there and telling them to take it someplace else. Don't worry. Just lock the door behind me. Okay? Don't worry, but lock the door."

We yelled and screamed for her to stay. She wouldn't listen. Little Judy even wrapped herself around Marisol's legs, but she eventually got her to let go.

"I've got my phone with me," she said. "If something happens, I can call the house phone. I'll pull the number up so it's ready. Probably this is nothing."

She unhooked the lock and pulled open the sliding glass door. Once it was closed behind her, she made sure we locked it. Then Marisol turned around to face the men in white who waited by the fire. We were all watching her from the window. She seemed so small. She seemed so brave. We could see her take a deep breath and then walk to the end of the deck, and then out into the yard and up the rise to where the men in white waited.

As she approached them, the men parted, as if to make room for her around the fire. Marisol had her arms crossed. She got up to the circle and said something.

"She doesn't look scared," Little Judy said. "I'd be so scared."

"I wonder what they're saying," Terrance said.

None of us knew, so none of us said anything. But the fact that they were talking made us feel better. Marisol had taken care of everything. This was all a misunderstanding. And she cleared it up.

Then, from the darkness at the edge of the yard, two more men in white appeared. They were behind Marisol, moving toward her.

"She can't see them!" Little Judy said.

"Somebody, do something," Slow Winston said and closed his eyes.

The men in white behind Marisol were crawling. Kind of crab-walking. And they kept moving closer.

Terrance pounded on the window.

Marisol turned to look back at the house. We could see she had a smile on her face, as if she was about to tell us that the whole thing had been a big mix-up. But then she saw the two men crab-walking behind her, and the smile dropped from her face.

One of the men lunged toward Marisol. He swung and hit her on the side of the head. He moved fast and with the robes, it was hard to tell exactly how it happened, but we could hear the crack from inside the house.

Marisol went down on one knee. She reached her hand out to the ground to steady herself. Her head wobbled. Then the other man who'd been crab-walking punched her on the cheekbone, and she fell over backwards so that her legs were folded underneath her.

The other men in white—the ones who'd been standing around the fire—didn't move. They just watched as the two crab-walkers grabbed her by the wrists and dragged her into the woods.

The darkness swallowed them up.

The whole thing lasted five seconds. We stepped back from the window and tried to understand what had just happened. We were alone in the house. The TV screen was still frozen on the big fat guy's face from *Fashion Police*.

"Maybe we should open the curtain," Terrance finally said, "because then at least we could see what they're doing."

"I don't want them looking at me," Little Judy said.

"We'll open it halfway," Terrance said. "You can stay behind that part, and I'll keep an eye on them."

"Like *you* could do anything about it anyway," Slow Winston said, but no one said anything back.

We decided to call Mom and Dad again from the kitchen phone. We dialed both their cellphones, plus a number we had for the Norwoods', but got no answer.

Just as we were about to dial 9-1-1, the phone rang. The little blue screen said, "Marisol A."

"That's her!" Little Judy shouted. "She's calling to tell us she's okay! Pick it up. Put it on speaker."

She sounded so convinced. And we wanted so badly for her to be right. Terrance pushed the button. We leaned in and listened.

From the first second the phone crackled to life, we realized everything was not okay. Nothing was okay.

There was a scraping sound, and then a sound of someone lifting a heavy weight. There was ragged breathing. Then we could hear Marisol, but she wasn't close to the phone.

"No, no, no," she said. "Why? Please. Why? God."

There were more sounds, and she said some more things but she was too far from the phone to understand. And then the phone cut off and the noise stopped.

"What are they doing?" Little Judy asked.

We looked at her, our young sister, and wondered if she knew, deep down, what was happening. Or if she *should* know. Even when you're going through the worst things, it's not always good to know.

"I think they're ghosts," Slow Winston said, even though that wasn't what we were talking about.

"No, that's not—"

Wham! Wham, wham!

We froze.

Bang! Bang, wham, wham!

It was the front door.

"Maybe it's the cops."

"Maybe it's more ghosts."

Wham, wham, wham!

We crawled down the hallway. We peeked around the corner and saw, through the side window, a bunch of kids standing on our porch. They were kids we knew, the ones we'd play Spud, and six different kinds of Tag, and Sardines, and Kick the Can, and Bloody Murder with.

Terrance opened the door and the kids all piled in. It was the McDaniels—Wanda, Wendell, and Walter. And it was the Orchards—Itsy, Zippy, and Pico. They were all talking at the same time, so it was hard to understand what was going on. But once we got them into the living room, they began to make sense.

"We were all together when we saw the sheet men," they said.

"So did we," we said.

"Then they lit a fire in the backyard."

"Exactly!" we shouted.

"And we tried to get help, but no one would come."

"Same here."

"So Denise went out to see what they wanted, but they took her."

We could tell by their grim faces that Denise had met the same fate as Marisol.

"What do we do now?" Pico Orchard asked.

We all looked at each other.

"Let's hide," Little Judy finally said. "We can go up to the attic and put a big trunk over the door and they'll never be able to get us."

"We'd be sitting ducks."

"Trapped."

"What if they decided to set the house on fire?"

"I don't hear you guys coming up with any ideas," Little Judy said. We could tell she was embarrassed by how hers had been shot down.

"We could ignore them," someone said.

"Should we call our parents again?"

"Maybe the police?"

"We could go on the roof and spell out *Help* with bedsheets."

"That's for floods."

Then it was quiet for a long time. No one had any more ideas.

We looked out the window again. The men in white were still there, standing around the fire. The wind was blowing and the bottoms of their robes flapped like clothes hanging on a line. There were five in our backyard, but we knew there were more. In the woods, hiding, waiting.

"We could fight back." It was Terrance who said this. He was the oldest of all the kids, and that made us listen.

"There's too many of them," Wendell McDaniel said.

"That's what Denise tried to do," Zippy Orchard said.

"They might be ghosts anyway," Slow Winston said. "How do you fight ghosts?"

"Hold on." Terrance ran upstairs and came down a minute later with his aluminum baseball bat, the one he used to hit a homerun in the game against Interstate Bank last year.

It was Little Judy who spoke first. "Pink Terrance, don't you even dare think about going out there."

"I'm just Terrance now, Little Judy."

"No one has to go out there," we all said. "There's no rule."

"We can't just sit here," Terrance said.

"Why not?" we asked.

"Because they're coming for us. Sooner or later. They're coming. We can't hide forever."

We yelled and pleaded. We screamed and grabbed his arms and legs and tried to drag him back to the couch. But he had grown a lot in the last year, and he was stronger than we'd realized.

He peeled us off. He told us everything would be all right. He told us that once they realized he meant business they'd probably get scared and run. He said that's what bullies do, and the men in white were nothing more than big bullies. He said we could help Marisol once we chased the men in white away and that, eventually, Mom and Dad would come back and we would barely remember this whole thing, like it was a bad dream that was only half there when you wake up.

This made us feel better. It gave us hope. We stopped yelling.

And he went. He slid open the back door. He closed it behind him. We locked it. We watched him turn around to face the men in white.

He shifted the baseball bat from one hand to the other. He took a step toward the edge of the deck.

That was when we saw a gray blur. Almost like a cloud or a puff of smoke. It started from the right and whizzed across the window. It seemed like it surrounded Terrance and picked him up and threw him off the deck to the left. It moved so fast Terrance didn't even have time to use his bat. We couldn't even tell what got him. But we knew what it meant, knew Terrance had been taken, knew he was gone.

We huddled in the living room, looking out the window, watching the men in white while they stood in our backyard watching us. There were too many of us to all fit on the couch, so some of us huddled on the floor. When the gray cloud took Terrance, none of us screamed. Maybe we knew something like that was bound to happen, and we were ready for it.

The TV screen clicked over to the screensaver. It started showing pictures of different places from way high above them. First it was a city with tall buildings, then a wide river valley, then a desert with sandy dunes that stretched on forever. Some of the youngest kids were crying, even Little Judy. But none of us said anything. There was nothing left to say.

It was Slow Winston who finally came up with the solution. No one expected it to come from him, but he was the next oldest, even counting the McDaniels and the Orchards, so maybe he was in the best position to figure it out.

When he told us the plan, it didn't make any sense. So he kept explaining it until we understood. It wasn't the best solution, wasn't what any of us would have wanted, but it didn't feel like we had a choice. So we quietly agreed.

We all lined up, biggest to smallest. From Slow Winston down to little Pico Orchard. We unlocked the back door and pulled it open wide. No one said a word. We walked out, and we didn't even bother to close the door behind us. The air smelled like smoke, from the fire. But we could smell something else too, something sharp in the air, like the smell of metal.

We stepped off the deck, still lined up in order. If you were watching from far away, you might think we were playing a game, but we weren't. We walked like that through the backyard.

The men in white who stood by the fire just watched us go by. As we got to the edge of the yard, we could hear sounds coming from the woods. Other kids, from other houses, crying. There were other sounds too. Adults making growls and grunts and yips and yowls. We knew now what waited for us in there. But what else could we do? We kept going. We marched straight into the woods, because we knew, as sure as anything, that we had no other choice.

The Solitude of

Jamiece Adams

When I was a child my mom slept through hours as easy as a river bends, a slow winding sleep. No matter the hour she would lay her head on a lace pillow, tuck down deep into floral pink sheets that tampered light streaming through the attic window, and be still. While I would be alone. I had to be about four because I had not been to school yet. It was right after my birthday that we had moved into Grandma's house. When my mom had finally left my father.

My father. The addict. My father, who couldn't pay rent, who crashed Mom's car, towed it under her name, and charged the fees to her credit card. Father. F-a-t-h-e-r. Just another name, another assortment of letters for a liar. I grew into my adulthood hating myself for continuing to love him. For thinking he might be someone different one day. I wonder if that's what painted the walls of my mom's dreams? Curated images of the man she thought she was seeing. The man that made us breakfast while singing off key in his boxers. The tall tower of perfect pastel light that danced with us in our apartment parking lot, who held my hand completely covered by his palm, while he unlocked the door. My father.

Often when she left me to sleep I'd sit in a tiny red chair. I'd watch a large-tube television, making sure to keep the volume just loud enough to catch every other word. I'd go outside and climb the trees in the backyard. I'd move through the house pretending I was an explorer. My Hot Wheels cars would race up and down the banisters. I'd jump the last three steps of the stairs that lead up to the attic. If several hours had gone, by I'd sit at the edge of our bed and stare at my mom's shape through the bedding. Trace the outline of her body in the air with my hand, wondering if she were alive. Beneath the fabric, could she breathe? Was there enough oxygen in her cocoon of blankets? To focus, I would hold my breath and remain still. I would lock my eyes on the area where her chest should have been, and wait. The pressure of my own need to survive would build in my lungs. I'd see the rise of the comforter like a slow yawn, mouth opening wide, then closing. Then I, too, would breathe.

She didn't tell me anything before we left him. We packed up what would fit in her rusted-out Toyota and drove away. I imagine it was raining, but I don't really know. The feeling of leaving is what sticks the most. A surprise collapse, a sinkhole appearing in the middle of my life, where none was before. I understood we weren't going back. What I couldn't understand was why she slept.

I learned from medical dramas that sleep could heal the body. Comas are induced to protect the brain from further trauma. But her body had not been harmed. She hadn't been thrown from a car window or fallen out a burning building. There were no scars on her skin, but what I didn't know was that there were many in places she kept covered. In places she couldn't even see.

On the third morning after the sleep started, I thought she would never rise for breakfast again. Grandma and I were in the kitchen. Her long blue nightdress kissed the floor as she moved about the cabinets, her hair in tight rollers. I always thought her skin looked peanut-butter brown like you could scrape a knife across her forearm and spread it on toast. I had slept in one of my father's black T-shirts, perfumed in pine and Irish Spring soap.

"June, baby girl, do you want sausage?" she asked.

"Bacon," I answered.

"Oatmeal?"

"No," I said to my lap.

"Eggs with cheese?"

Her questions stopped. I looked up. Mom was standing in the kitchen doorway.

"She's got cereal. I bought it before we, um, well, before we got here." She said this to the peeling yellow-painted walls. To the cracked white ceiling, the gray tiled floor. Sleep marked her face. Deep circling rings under her eyes like a redwood cut through the core.

I watched her gather the simple ingredients even after Grandma insisted on making us breakfast. Mom's hair was loosely clipped to the back of her head. She moved around the kitchen in her tattered Lakers jersey, nodding and saying it wasn't a problem. I wanted to touch the loose hairs at the nape of her neck like she'd do for me when I was sick.

Instead, I looked at my small hands and my feet not even long enough to touch the kitchen floor, useless. I didn't see it happen, but the sound drew my eyes to the floor. Against the gray tile were pieces of a white ceramic bowl.

"I'm just tired," she admitted. She apologized. But I thought, how could that be? After days of rest, a person shouldn't feel sleepy anymore. This had to be something else. Grandma swept the mess away while Mom left the kitchen. I watched her shadow darken even as the morning light shone through the open windows. I missed her in a way I never had, felt a darkness of my own settle. Grandma poured me a bowl of cereal before she left to check on Mom. I tried to shake off the chill that rolled through me, but it stayed. I fought back at the feeling to nap, afraid of what might happen if I let sleep take me.

The closest I felt to Mom in those days was during bath time. The water would be so hot that my skin would tingle as she lowered me into the tub. Once my feet had gotten used to the heat I would kneel, then sit, then lie on my back to wet my hair. Mom knelt next to the tub, her head on the porcelain edge, possibly daydreaming. She'd skim her fingers across the water-like tadpoles. After I had submerged my entire body, I'd stand. She was so tender. The washcloth moving across my legs, my arms, my pot-belly stomach that she would poke, and I would laugh, her half smile was enough in that moment. After washing my tightly curled hair, she would pour a cup of water over my head, my eyes closed tight. The streams of warmth felt like fingers brushing down my face over and over. Once she was done, still with my eyes closed, she would wrap me in a towel. She'd take me from the tub into her lap. While she sat on the lid of the toilet, she would hold me close to her body.

I'd look up at her faraway face and say, "I love you."

"I love you too," she whispered.

These moments were rare. Eventually, bathing me would come less frequent, sleep consuming her, undercurrents of sorrow pulling her beneath the pain. It diverged from the middle, where a hollow ache of hunger sat, where the melancholy had infected her the most.

There's this story my mom tells me. She always starts by asking, do you remember when your father took you? And each time, I tell her no. When I was young, he used to take me places all the time. He would take me to the park to play in the trees. We would go to a pond in the winter and skip rocks across the surface, trying to find a soft spot to take them beneath the water. But Mom was not referring to any of that. She was asking about the time he took me all day without telling her.

Back before she left him for good. When cell phones were a luxury that most people couldn't afford. He hadn't told her where we were going. He left while she was at work. Mom called his family and hers. No one knew where we were. She said that when he finally came home she was mortified. She said, "Your face was dirty, there was a hole in your white stockings, and you smelled like mildew. I slapped him across the face and took you to my chest to hold you. I could have killed him right there, but I was just so relieved. June, I thought you would never come home. I told him he would never take you again, ever. You were so young, but you knew that something hadn't been right. Before he took you, you would get up with him and make breakfast, dance with him in your PJs before bedtime . . . you stopped doing that for weeks, and then it was like you forgot what happened. But not me, I never did."

Mom tells me this story every chance she gets, I think, hoping I will remember something from that day. Sometimes, in my mind, I call up pretend people, tall figures. Dark shades of nondescript human outlines, like cutout paper dolls, but all imagined.

My grandma called Aunt Victoria when Mom stopped eating consistently. Her son, Jacob, my cousin, came with her. I didn't particularly like him, but it was a relief to have company after weeks of being alone. Jacob's thick round glasses and curly hair tickled my face as he whispered his new game in my ear.

"Let's play spy. My mom and your mom are the enemies. So we have to follow them, and you'll have to follow me."

I nodded with as much interest as a fish in a glass bowl. The screen door whined open. I could hear voices. We jogged to the bathroom across the hall from the attic.

"Victoria, you don't have to keep telling me over and over again," Mom said.

She and Aunt Victoria went to the kitchen. The refrigerator door opened. Glasses of beer clinked, echoing through the house. I pointed upstairs to the attic. Jacob shook his head and motioned for me to stay. I didn't. Tiptoeing across the front room, I took the stairs two at a time, avoiding the loose floorboards. Jacob seemed to press on every creak and crack. I ushered him into the closet. Left it cracked so that we could still see our parents. The dark pressed its hand on my back. I bit back fear with my teeth. Their voices grew closer.

"He said he would go to rehab, get better, and I believed him for so long, too long," my mom said. Her voice was soft, as if sandpaper had taken all her edges and smoothed her out. Through the tiny slit in the closet door, I saw them sit in the bed with their knees touching. I watched the lean in their backs and the bend of their legs. Sisterhood reached between them, coils of love searching for comfort.

"Honey, we all fall for the wrong people. My psychic told me that it's the way the world keeps balanced. The bad has to happen so the good can happen too," Victoria said.

"No one needs a psychic to tell them that," Mom snapped.

Aunt Victoria pursed her lips, annoyed. Mom put her head in her hands. Jacob poked me in the back. I swatted his hand away, also annoyed, but then I saw it, on the bed my mom's shadow grew darker, deepening the line of her entire body. It stretched and snapped back and forth with the movement of her hands.

"Do you see that?" I whispered to Jacob.

"I can barely see anything with your head in the way," he whispered back. I kneeled and pointed to the bed. Barely notable in the dark closet was the shrug of his shoulders. I turned back to the bed, but the light from the attic window shone only on the sheets.

"I just don't understand how I didn't notice everything from the start." Mom's eyes were wet when she looked up. It made my own sting.

I'd seen my mother cry before then. Sort of, if you count movies and small infants at the mall. But this cry was framed with tight skin bunched at the edges with grief. I didn't want to watch anymore. I slid to the back of the closet and waited for them to leave the room. Jacob left me there. Closed the closet door completely. I thought eventually I would panic, but I sat still among the musty coats and old Christmas wrapping paper. The dark no longer frightened me.

For a while I thought Dad would come for us. That he would knock on the door wearing his favorite green flannel I picked out for his birthday. He'd take us back home, then Mom would stay awake all day again. It didn't take long for me to realize that wasn't going to happen. He never called, or if he did, he never asked to speak to me. I was forgotten in the midst of the broken pieces of their life. Grandma did her best, but she was busy trying to help Mom. I think they thought I was too young to understand. But I did understand, I saw everything. Dad was gone. I felt it when his voice became more like a recording in my head. When the smell of his soap evaporated into generic brand detergent, his face only captured on a picture I kept hidden from Mom in my sock drawer. On some level, even then, I knew I had to act ok, so everyone else could heal.

I counted to three and jumped. My glee quickly turned into panic when I slipped and hit my knee on the hardwood. I froze. I had made too much noise jumping down the stairs. The thump shook the walls. The pain of hitting my knee was secondary to the fear of waking up Mom. It happened only a few times before. The threat always a tight arm grab accompanied by a tired, but tense, "I'll make you sleep too." I didn't want that sleep, not her long, despondent stillness that went on until the sun either rose or dipped entirely into the ground.

The sound of her feet striking the attic floor radiated irritation. It echoed outward, following her footsteps down the stairs. She grabbed me by the arm and dragged me into the bed. I cried, my back against the wall pleading to be let back to my own pleasures, my own seclusion.

"If I wake up and you aren't here, I will spank you. That's a promise," she said from within her cocoon of fabric.

My sobs eventually slowed to hiccup-like sniffling. It was still so bright outside. The light beamed into the room so brilliantly that I couldn't see what was beyond the window. The attic was somehow covered in its own silhouette ; night had made its home here. I let the tears dry to my skin. The streaks would stand out white and chalky on my cheeks. I wanted her to see what she had done, that the closest my eyes would get to her dark rings were the tears stained on my face. I stiffened at the thought of being dragged into her slumber. Then, in slow quakes, defiance gripped my muscles. Disobedience, sluggish and thick, moved my back away from the wall. Choking down a panicked breath, I moved from under the cover. Breaking off my skin was a feeling like the snap of weak rubber bands. I was afraid. With my eyes low, I crawled carefully to avoid my mother's body curled tight. If she woke up, I wanted to at the very least make it to the end of the bed.

I felt the cool wood floor on my toes, then on the balls of my feet. I looked up to see her sleeping. Every groan of the floorboards pushed me forward until my bare feet touched the concrete outside the front door.

The day was warm with summer, the air blithe, playing with my braided hair. The grass, somehow still wet with dew, cooled my feet warmed by the concrete. I picked up fuzzy white dandelions and blew them like they were eyelashes, wishing. I blew them stronger than birthday candles, softer than a prayer. I watched them fly like unstrung balloons. Some went to the sky, lost in blue, others floated back to the lawn, but most met their end on the windshield of a bright yellow pickup truck. Watching those made my knees buckle, sad because now I knew even the wind could take the wrong turn.

Heading back inside, I tripped over an uneven piece of concrete and slid across the gravel. Bits of beige and black stuck to my legs with bright reds and peeled brown skin. I limped back to the attic. I pulled myself into the bed. The mattress cradled me in cotton. Exhaustion felt native. My body failed to resist. I had forgotten what lay next to my mother cradled in the dark of her body. Bands seemed to tighten around me like the legs of a dying insect. I felt sleep on the cusp, fading my conscious thoughts to black.

I was aware of a tickle. It spread down my spine looping around the shelf of each rib. The area behind my eyelids had become a solid space, an eclipsed landscape. There was no sky. There were no trees. I felt the weight of myself. I saw the back of my mother's body shrouded in black smoke at a great distance.

June.

She walked backward toward me. The back of her head acted as a new face, but distance never changed, pushed back by slabs of concrete every inch gained lost . So I walked forward. *Mom.* Tar lashed around my legs, making each step impossible. By the time I was an arm's reach away from her heels, my stomach was flesh with the ground. The tar worked its way like vines across my limbs. My fingernails broke, bloody with the effort of pulling myself closer and closer. I opened my mouth to shout her name. The letters bulged in my throat, impeding my breath. With one last push, I brushed the bare skin of her ankle.

I awoke from sleep blinking back the fatigue. My eyes formed the shapes of the attic and I saw Mom praying on her knees beside the bed. I could not see her face. She was pleading for God to help her let go of the things that she could not control and the wisdom to know the difference. I held my breath to keep quiet. Desperately I wanted to tell her that I hurt, too, but I knew she was not really there. That she would not understand when her pain had taken her so far from me. Resentment bubbled up in my stomach acid like baking soda to vinegar. This person was not my mom. I rolled over, unable to watch anymore. The black that hid her face was too accurate a representation of the person who lived in daylight.

In moments alone when silence feels heavy, I think about those days, and how that could be me. I think of the dream. Of the dried blood I found under my fingernails the next morning. I fight at the tiredness growing in my bones, pushing through long days. Sleep is a constant reminder that I could become a stranger to my own life.

When my mom calls, we never talk extensively about that time. A great deal of unresolved resentment closes me off. But one day I had to know. Exhausted with my head in my free hand, I had to know if she knew that sorrow could take her away. If she knew that the fabric of her life could collapse with one strong pull. If she ever thought it could happen again. Could she sleep like that again?

She let the air on the line thicken. I waited for the image, called up from my mind and ghosted in spreading smoke, of her back, of the tar spreading, of bloody nails, of my throat, of the light, of the growing shadow. Her voice cut through the memories and halted the surge of dread in my chest.

Simply, she said, "Some parts of ourselves remain unknown until they aren't."

True enough, but it didn't help ease my thoughts about sleep. After we hung up, I imagined her in the kitchen or standing on her back porch. Sitting at her small dining-room table. Swinging in the hammock I put up in her backyard, anywhere, anywhere but her bedroom.

Human Kneads

J. A. Bernstein

I never thought the idea of making love communally would be all that useful for a business, but then again, I'd only been living in Duluth, Minnesota, for a year.

My wife and I had moved to the city in August, where I'd restarted my studies, and my wife, who's from the area, suggested we get involved with a bakery, a so-called "cooperative," that a friend of a friend was trying to revive. I'll admit I was skeptical. My wife doesn't cook. And I was already overwhelmed with tasks, from refinishing our floors and maintaining the dilapidated wreck of a house that we'd bought near downtown to finishing my homework each night—I settled on criminology, which would later prove useful, given the folks with whom we worked. Even the bakery was collapsing. The oven didn't work, the floor needed tiles, the sinks and stove had to be gutted, all of which I thanklessly did while my wife took her turn playing the part of the domestic—three hours brushing rolls, two more stirring creams, a few minutes here and there to do icing, which Roderick, the fuck, helped her do. Not that I'm bitter. It was a fruitful operation. We were two of twelve in the gig, and frankly things were going amicably until they decided—I emphasize they—that our bakery needed a "hook."

It started on a Saturday. I'd just swung by Home Depot to pick up some caulk, and, upon approaching the corner of Fourth, which is where I normally parked, I found a strange van lurking next to the shop: an enormous, blue, half-peeling Dodge whose cabin was vaguely stenciled A.C. Heating & Gas. Since I'd just installed the boiler myself and even had the City come down to inspect it, I had no idea why it was there. But

I faintly realized something was awry when I noticed the Led Zeppelin shirt tied to the rearview. My wife despises Led Zeppelin, though I've always been a fan.

Our bakery was—I emphasize was—located in one of the dicier parts of town, East Hillside. The neighborhood had at one time been populated by millionaires, back when the grain mills still churned, ore was shipping in, and the timber mills ran at full mast. Now the area consisted chiefly of homeless—how they survive in Duluth, I don't know—and halfway houses, into which the mansions had been ignobly converted. The place smelled of Dumpsters and lice, not to mention the ever-present rain that engulfed it. Even in January, when the regional temperatures hit negative forty, somehow East Hillside barely dipped below freezing—it might have been the effect of the power plant just up the street—and the result was a residual, light, dripping slush, not unlike the glaze my wife began applying to buns. I emphasize began.

When I approached the bakery, the first thing I noticed was that the windows were curtained, and a small line had formed by the door. These weren't the usual Saturday-morning shoppers. No wearied fathers with infants in tow, no tawny tourists sporting Duluth Packs. No, these folks were scraggly—bearded, like me—in vintage, fur-collared coats or ankle-length, brown leather jackets. One woman, whose neck was tattooed and barely visibly beneath her blue scarf, wore a vintage pea coat, not unlike Audrey Hepburn's, and nibbled a long cigarette.

"Greetings," I said.

Nobody replied.

I'll admit I hadn't gotten out much. Between work and school, I rarely visited The Lounge, a bar up the street, where my wife and the other bakers often went, and where alt-country and cover bands performed, most doing shoddy impersonations of Dylan. Why we'd even come to Duluth I didn't know, though the housing was cheap, tuition was affordable, and my wife had her parents nearby, who were less of a burden than I'd supposed. Plus, we were planning to have kids soon—as soon as I finished my degree—and, assuming the bakery didn't take off, I'd get a job in corrections, which had always been a minor goal, if not my loftiest dream.

Inside, the bakery was dark—too dark, I thought—and the unmistakable sound of Led Zeppelin's "Kashmir" rang from the back: "Talk in song from tongues of lilting grace / Sounds caress my ear."

Beside the display case with honey rolls, which I had also installed, and the overpriced cookies we peddled, two women were going at it, both locked in sumptuous embrace. They were still clothed—one in a flimsy sundress, the other a ragged fur coat, which enshrouded them both—and both lay pressed against the glass. I couldn't make out either face, though long locks of auburn hair streamed out from the coat.

Beside them, a tall Japanese man in faded blue overalls appeared to be smoking a pipe, while Claire, our associate, was fumbling with the iMac's credit card swipe. The place had gotten crowded, and a couple more hipsters were raising their phones, apparently trying to record.

"Where's Laur?" I asked Claire, referring to my wife. Claire smiled at me gingerly. A ruffling ensued in the coat, and then, beside the display case, beside the snickerdoodles I had just baked, and which we sold for a full three-and-a-half dollars a pop, my wife emerged with her lips against somebody else. She smiled a bit deferentially and pushed the young woman aside.

The crowded stirred, as if I had interrupted the show.

"Hey, sweet," said Claire, as if speaking for my wife. "Laura's busy. But I want you to meet Zuriñe."

Zuriñe, whom I knew was half-Spanish, and who wasn't unattractive, albeit rounded in parts, had begun working at the bakery this week. She studied eco-lit at the college and was an adamant vegan, which is why the snickerdoodles tasted like dust. Our shifts hadn't overlapped, but as an owner of the cooperative, I'd been apprised of her hire, as well as her culinary needs.

"Laur," I begged half-insistently. "What is going on?"

Zuriñe tried to hug Laura, who still shied away, less embarrassed, it seemed, than confused. Then Laura, strangely enough, reached out for a tray of glazed sticky buns. "Here, dear. I made these for you."

Before she could pass them over, however, the crowd began staking its claim.

My first instinct was: what had I done? Failed to satisfy her lately? Waited too long to have kids? Sure, my hours were long at the college, and she'd had little to do beside mope around the bakery and come up with delicate buns. Worse, she took to The Lounge, where she'd obviously met Zuriñe.

"I'm sorry," said my wife, licking her thumb, munching on a delectable treat. "We were just having a . . . snack." She smiled at me lovingly, knowingly in fact, as if I shouldn't be jealous or mad. I knew my wife had fooled around a bit in college—she had studied at Madison, and unlike me, was incredibly, eerily smart. I also knew better than to act the part of the cuckold, especially in an aura like this, so I reached for a sticky bun, having parted the crowd, and said, "Okay, that's cool."

Zuriñe, by the way, in case it wasn't clear, lived in the refurbished van. How she heated it in winter, I still didn't know, though I'm guessing my wife would find out.

One of the difficulties in manning a small business operation, or so said Jamaal, our Business Associate—who, by the way, never set foot in the place—was securing advertising pledges and promoting your message abroad. We couldn't depend on tourists, who were plentiful in summer but disappeared as soon as the snow, or slush, as it were, began to fall. As part of our campaign to "spread awareness," I began distributing fliers and taping up posters in shops. "Try our Love Brownies. You've never known such delectable warmth." Or: "Non-cumbersome Muffins. All the sweetness, with none of the flakes." Soon our messages became even less subtle. "Stop in Saturday, Nov. __, for the baking event of your life. Chocolate gooey richness, no questions asked. 21+."

I will say this about Duluth: The town is comparably tolerant. Unlike Superior across the bay, where they practically stone fornicators, Duluth has a thriving gay community, pays for recycling, and generally tolerates bikes—that is, for the three months of the year when they're rideable. It is also for these reasons that a small hipster community has formed. What these folks do, I don't know. Like most, I suppose, they have trust funds. But they began congregating nightly at The Lounge, and before that, the bakery, which became the most happening place. Can I say happening? Is that the appropriate term? I grew up on a farm, and though I relocated a lot when my dad left, I was never cool enough to like Dylan or the rest of these alt-country bands. Which is probably why I'm stuck with Led Zeppelin.

I came home about a week after this kissing debacle to find my wife in bed, enshrouded in blankets, a glass of wine in hand, giggling uproariously. At first I thought she was masturbating—it wouldn't be the first time that I caught her, which sometimes provoked something else—but rather she was gripping a frayed orange book. It was *The Idiot*, by Dostoevsky, which I couldn't recall having seen.

"The City's getting on us about the boiler," I said. "They're looking to dig up a fine. I should never have let Roderick try to install it, let alone do it mys—"

"Honey, come lie down with me." My wife looked at me placidly. She was visibly drunk, and I didn't want to get involved.

"I'm drunk but truthful," she said, leafing through the novel.

Uncorking the bottle: "Do you want to talk about your new woman-friend, Zuriñe?"

"She's just a kid. Besides, she likes Zeppelin. You're the only one that I love." She rose to hug me, and I took a swig of the wine.

For some reason, the only words that came to mind, words I didn't say, were: *Talk in song from tongues of lilting grace / Sounds caress my ear.* "Duluth Packs is littered with fliers," I finally mumbled. "So's Fitger's Pub."

She looked at me softly. "Do you want to have kids?"

"Not really," I said, with a smile.

I should have seen it coming. I mean, all of us should, all of us who wed in our youth. I'd met Laur in college when I was hauling her futon, and we'd hooked up one night at a pub. I hadn't been with a lot of women before her. In fact, I wasn't very popular in school, wasn't much of an athlete, nor much of a scholar to be sure. At the time I was working my way through Eau Claire, mostly doing floors and odd jobs. Tuition was unaffordable, even then. I was just looking for an educated woman, and that she seemed to be. Her folks were doctors—psychiatrists, in fact—and she'd grown up along the North Shore, about a dozen clicks north of Duluth, in a spacious log cabin, which, of course, her father had had built. They were country-folks, or trying to be, and I admired them for that goal, since I, who had had the roof taken away from over me at least six or seven times (I followed my mother to Wyoming, then Utah, then back to Wisconsin, where she finally found a man she could love), had never much warmed to the city, or the rich folks who people that place.

Laur, when I first met her, looked beautiful to me: large, copper eyes; radiant hair; generous bosom; thin wrists. She was a little heavy in the middle—all of us are—and her forehead was narrowly lined, suggesting to me that she'd read, or at least was wise for her age. She'd studied English at Madison and considered writing fiction but was afraid of "pursuing that path." She just wanted a "normal life, not a writer's," she said, that evening at the High Noon Saloon, where some indie band was playing. Ass Cobra, I think they were called. She sipped her Stroh's and gripped the pine table, leaning close to my ear. "You seem like a normal person. Not like these folks." We were seated upstairs in a balconied section, beneath which some moshers now spun.

"I've never been here."

She leaned into my face. Her copper eyes glimmered. She put my hand to her hair. "Do you want to go work on that futon?"

"Why not? Ass Cobra isn't too great."

She smiled at me softly—that same one she'd later make when I told her I'd handed out fliers.

And here we were on a Friday, prepping the joint, if joint is the word I can use. Though the bakery's exterior had been done up before in a late-forties style, with its original clapboard façade, acrylic red awning, and turquoise wood cutaways denoting our previous name—Like a Rolling Scone—we officially re-registered as Love's Bakery and Social Club, and the turquoise was replaced with a peculiar, almost lavender, pink.

"Are we creating a brothel?" I had asked, inspecting the shade at Home Depot. "Zuriñe's my friend," Laur explained.

At least it was out in the open, this thing, though she and I had barely spoken throughout the month. I had had exams, not to mention a leaking roof amidst a surge of fresh hail, and Laura was recruiting new hires, whatever that entailed. She had spent Tuesday and Wednesday nights of that week away from our home—I didn't ask where—and came back with a chill and runny nose.

Claire had spent the week devising heart-shaped red bagels, which I didn't think possible, and may have not been entirely natural, as was her wont, though didn't seem to run afoul of Zuriñe. Roderick , who lifted weights in his free time and mildly resembled an ox, both in size and in temperament, went to work installing new lights, which he did with the precision and care that I imagine a hooved animal would take. The result was a kind of blinking, half-reddened interior—I believe the bulbs were chromium—and not unlike a beating heart, which I immediately had to rewire. Our display case was replaced with an antique Chesterfield couch, which they'd somehow lugged from the Goodwill. And the small seating area, which had formerly contained a few stools and scuffed tables looking out onto Fourth, made way for what I can only describe as bleachers, or a makeshift array of wood piers. These were covered with brushed velvet—also from Goodwill—and an assortment of mounted trays (suffice it to say Roderick had had a long week). I had no doubt the seating would collapse and probably kill a few people, assuming the bagels didn't get to them first.

Am I being bitter? Possibly I am. Or was. Because when the crowds began arriving that night—yes, night; folks actually camped on the street—for The Event the next morning, which they'd appropriately dubbed "Human Kneads," I began to take umbrage at my wife. Not because she was sleeping with someone else; I could care less (or, at least, let's pretend for a second that's true); but that she was indubitably right. All week, the bakery had been raking in sales. We'd sold out of sticky buns, or "Love Rolls," as we called them. Breads were backordered, and by Thursday, the oven conked out. Fortunately, Roderick and Jamaal had had the brilliant idea of outsourcing most of the goods—they had contacts at two other local bakeries, both Scandinavian and relics of an era long gone. Come Friday morning, Zuriñe's van had been filled and unloaded at least seven times, mostly with "Love Bars," our signature dish, a kind of gooey, red substance layered with crumbs, and in which, it was rumored, Roderick had sprinkled ample doses of Intrinsa, which may or may not have been legal in Canada.

I first noticed the gatherers that Friday, since they weren't our typical crowd. The vintage clothing was replaced with new, upmarket brands—Canada Goose, Patagonia—and the shoppers themselves were not young. Mostly middle-agers, even some elderly types. Barely a soul under fifty. They said they were visiting from Bismarck, Detroit. One couple drove an RV from Tampa, which, in November, I couldn't believe. All had been apprised of an occurrence this Saturday and wanted to get a good seat. Oh, and could they try the Love Bars? I guess the Yelp reviews were off the charts.

I also began to wonder how long the authorities would stay away, but soon the fire crew showed up, then the police team, as well, and asked if they could get some good seats. Oh, and maybe some bars for their friends.

The few folks who did camp out that night—there were only two or three—were relatively young—in their mid-forties—and Roderick agreed to let them sleep in the shop, where they may or may not have been treated to some of his signature bars.

I went home that night and helped myself to a drink—a couple, to be sure—and worked on resealing our roof. I'd done well enough on my tests—aced Crime Prevention, though only pulled a "B" in Social Structures, having boggled the Chicago School—and didn't much care to ask where my wife had since gone. At around midnight, however, I got a call from her folks, who asked if I could pick her up. Apparently, she had arrived in a fit, passed out on their couch, and woke up, cursing my name. Why they'd bother to call wasn't clear, though I'd begun to suspect they trusted me more than her.

"Sure thing," I explained, not looking forward to braving 61 in my truck, in which the heating didn't work, and even less to hearing the tale of where she had been.

"I'm sorry," she growled, as the door to the cabin flung open, and out she sprang wearing her coat—the new (vintage) fur one. I tried to hug her. She stepped inside our Ram. "I hope the fucking heater's working."

Returning, cowled like a monk in her coat, she explained that she'd had a fight with Zuriñe. Wasn't a big deal, but she didn't feel comfortable with her. She said she "loved her husband the most" and "wasn't into these things." It had just been "an experiment," that's all. "Zuriñe was really cool, and she encouraged my writing. But I told her I'm married. That's it. And when I explained to her I was pregnant—"

"You're what?"

Her copper eyes flickered. "Oh yeah. By the way."

I gazed ahead at the sleeted expanse of the road.

In Dostoevsky's *The Idiot*, which I've subsequently read, a young Russian prince returns home after having spent four years abroad recovering in a Swiss sanitarium. He finds himself surrounded by scoundrels and knaves, among whom, ironically enough, he remains the shrewdest one. At one point, the narrator—I presume a stand-in for Dostoevsky—begins lashing out at the people of his place and time. "Many of our young women have thought fit to cut their hair short, put on blue spectacles, and call themselves Nihilists. By doing this they have been able to persuade themselves, without further trouble, that they have acquired new convictions of their own."

I'm trying to imagine what my wife might have seen in this book, what she found hysterical. After all, she was friends with Zuriñe, Claire, Roderick, the rest, and if my wife couldn't see through them, which I'm sure she must have done, it's hard to see how anyone could.

That night, eight hours before "Human Kneads," with my wife now snoring in our bed, I found myself restless, unable to sleep, and decided to go for a drive. It wasn't the thought of having a child that unnerved me. In a strange way, I'd warmed to the thought, however quickly it had ensued. Rather, I remained puzzled as to what my associates had planned, or how they'd coopted my wife. I sought some counsel, or the closest thing, at The Lounge up the street from our shop.

"I think it's kinda spooky," said Claire, my associate, whom I found in a booth near the back. It also wasn't lost on me (later) that her head had been shaved, though it was Roderick, at the bar, wearing spectacles, less blue than dark green, and of the sort Groucho Marx donned. "I mean, a lot of us were fooling around," she explained. "Nothing really serious. You know, just kisses in back, a few pokes here and there by the sink"—I winced—"but your wife, no, she wasn't down. She and Zuriñe, they kind of went their own way, and I guess it came to fruition that Saturday, the morning you walked in. I can't account for it. She isn't that type. And she loves you, I know," Claire sighed.

I sipped my ale, which was apparently unfiltered and resembled somebody's waste. "Well, that's good to know."

"She wasn't even keen on 'Human Kneads,' or whatever they're calling it." Claire glanced up at Roderick, who was sliding tickets down the bar in exchange for a thick wad of cash. Behind him, a Led Zeppelin cover band was playing—seriously—and Chinese lanterns hung beside the musty brick wall. The place had been a warehouse formerly and still smelled of dehydrated fish, though that might have been the T-shirt Claire wore. Beyond her, the front room was mobbed, despite the ring of last call. "Frankly, I'm not too into it either. It was Roderick's idea. And Jamaal's. It seems to me a guy-thing . . . and degrading, really, to girls. But I'll tell you the truth: we all need the tuition. And I guess you've got a child on the way."

I watched her sulkily.

"Congratulations, by the way."

"In my thoughts I have seen," wailed the black woman-vocalist, tambourine in hand, "rings of smoke through the trees . . . And the voices of those who stand looking."

Communal, as I understand it, implies some kind of mutual exchange, or at least the tacit understanding that goods are being equally shared. In my course on macroeconomics, which I initially flunked, the textbook mentioned intentional communities, citing the Kibbutz as an example, and showing how all of them failed. This was for debated reasons—my guess is Mao had an answer, if not Claire herself—but the textbook, from what I recall, described the "problem of incentives," that is, what motivates a person to give and not just take. It's beyond me to dispute that. Suffice it to say that when I entered Love's Bakery and Social Club the next morning, sharing was not in effect.

Roderick, who evidently displayed ample prowess as a bodybuilder, stood stiffly in front of Lisa Ann, another associate, who was rubbing agave on his chest. His loincloth, I descried, passing beyond the manned doorway (a whole team of security was present, whom Jamaal had apparently hired, and the place was fully darkened, though packed to the brim with souls), consisted of some kind of sticky bun, which was carefully fastened with pins. To what it adhered I don't know—this doesn't speak well of his girth—and Lisa Ann, who knelt beside him on the rickety Chesterfield, was wearing a sequined dress, that, if I'm not mistaken, was lined in parts with granola, which she occasionally, languidly licked. The music, if one can call it that, was some kind of Gregorian chant, and I only realized the pertinence of that when Claire, clad in full nun's apparel, including tunic and coif, emerged from the kitchen bearing a tray full of dongs. They were shaped like éclairs but lacked chocolate icing and mushroomed a bit near the tips. The insides contained a gooey white cream, as the audience discovered, amidst loud applause, when one entered Claire's cupped throat.

"Love bars for sale," called the overalled Japanese man—the one who'd been sporting a pipe. Evidently he, too, had become an associate, making his rounds down the aisle.

Zuriñe, for her part, was nowhere to be seen. It's possible she, too, was sick, like my wife, or had also remained at home. This was just as well, since I probably would have spat in her face, or, worse, tried to undertake what Roderick now did to Lisa Ann. I won't describe it. Suffice it to say that copious amounts of custard were involved—jam filling, as well—and the crowd was fully enthused.

No one seemed to take notice of my entry. Which was just as well. Because when the first pipe began to blow in the basement downstairs, nobody paid me much heed.

I suppose my technical role was operations manager, handling, as I did, the facility equipment and repair. One of these tasks, undoubtedly, was ensuring that the boiler had been up to code. I'll admit—I'm writing "fiction" after all, as my wife would claim to do—that the left guardrail might not have been installed, and we'd had several other issues with compliance, though I doubt these can account for what occurred. Rather I like to think fate was behind it, or maybe just the heat in that place, which had undoubtedly risen with all of the baking that week, not to mention the display on our "stage." And, of course, I can't rule out the possibility that Zuriñe, or someone, was siphoning heat to her van.

The first rattling, I believe, shook the piers, discombobulating most of the viewers, who attributed it to the stage, where Lisa Ann was undoubtedly having a good time—Claire had since joined her, nun's habit and all—though the more likely explanation was the pressure valve warped, and the seating itself had come loose. This wouldn't become apparent, of course, to anyone in the venue but me, long after the crowd was dispersed and the bakery—or what was left of it—was fitfully, lawfully condemned.

I often wonder what the police must have thought—apparently licenses were acquired; leave it to Jamaal to have procured all the necessary permits, and in no short amount of time—when the boiler flew up through the stage, just beside Roderick, who was flexing and admiring his bicep. Whether he had achieved climax at that point— the groinal buns remained intact, even as the back floor dissolved all around him—remains a standing question. What isn't is the fate of our roof. In view of a hundred peering eyes, possibly more, a rusting cylinder shot through the tiles. It must have been three yards in width, twice that in length, and a solid ton in weight. That it had been jealous of Roderick, or dismissive of his size, also couldn't escape our view as it plunged through the air, like some hell-sputtered missile, and took half the ceiling with it, soaring up into space. Somebody screamed. White powder flew. Then the roof beams started to collapse.

In the stampede that followed—picture: naked limbs, globs of red jam, and granola bits whipping through air—I managed to make my way out, prying the back door and probably saving quite a few lives. Indeed, it was no small miracle—call it an act of grace, attributable, I'd guess, to Claire's robe—that nobody was seriously injured, at least inside our store. A few folks suffered burns—Roderick's arm was singed, and something else, which he wouldn't describe—and the bakery became a total loss. That's assuming that it hadn't been before.

As for where the boiler came down, that I can't say—after all, isn't fiction, unlike marriage, governed by laws or rules? Suffice it to say my wife's favorite lounge no longer serves unfiltered ale, or much of anything for that matter, though Led Zeppelin continues to play for whatever grim creatures emerge.

As for my wife, well, she ran away and is living, I suppose, in a van. I haven't inquired. Her folks are still here. She studies writing these days in L.A., joined, it would seem, by an acquaintance of herbivore taste. I know because the alimony bills include a grocery tab, which I can see. Her parents help us out. In fact, they've taken me on as a handyman up at their place. Whether their daughter will return, that I can't say, though I'm looking forward to meeting our child. And who knows? Maybe I'll teach him to read Dostoevsky. "I'm drunk but truthful," says Lebedeff, the rogue of the tale, after his wife is long gone.

The Secret of the Old Clockwork 'O'

A Nancy Droog, Ultraviolent Girl Detective Mystery

Meredith Counts

Chapter One

"What's it going to be, then, eh?" Nancy asked herself.

She was zipping fastlike down the road in the dark blue kabriolet avtomobil her father had bought her for her eighteenth birthday.

Nineteen now, and world weary, she cut that car through the countryside. Cheerfully grim, she was. She had seen too much but had come around to smiling about it anyway. The top was down.

The car was outfitted with a fine stereo so Beethoven's 4th pounded fast around the dangerous young sleuth then fluted in dreamy and slow then fast and mad once more. With one gloved hand responsibly on the wheel, Nancy flung her other hand up, stabbing the air ultrapreciselike to the music, conducting the darkened pines.

She jabbed the old air just like she had seen the Italian conductor do, back when her friend Allison Hoover took voice lessons with the famous music-lover who'd retired to their pleasant town of River Heights.

But that had been a long year ago, before Alison was murdered, before Nancy took her revenge and Nancy's father, the respected advokat Carson Droog had checked his daughter into a home of rest and reabilitatsiya for her dark thoughts and darker actions.

Under those fitted gloves were a pair of well-manicured hands, tidy and capable of unspeakable things.

It was a pleasant night for a drive. She reflected on all that happened in the past few years: being attacked by a dog, finishing high school, solving mysteries but relying too heavily on underaged slurps of Moloko Plus down by the picturesque Muskoka River to quiet the screeching nighttime truths of small-town crime. Nancy had never really known her own mother. They never talked about this at home.

She remembered the burglars locking her up in the cabin on Moon Lake last year, tossing Nancy in a closet there and leaving her for dead with the mothballs. The missing letter could still be there. Allison's death had interrupted Nancy's investigation.

After Allison's murder junior year, Nancy got to know the seamy underbelly of River Heights firsthand, beyond her father's lawyerly dinner-table gossip, and made new acquaintances. She joined a fine gang of bloodthirsty young women, maybe not as bent on justice as Nancy herself but always ready for the knockdown dragouts. Nancy's chickclik were no students of opera, though when they went about their business Nancy was known to have an earbud filling her skull with old Ludwig Van between her efficient kicks and jabs.

She was excited for a reunion. It was a fortunate thing that her father had paid to have her car tuned up after she'd had a wreck. It drove almost the same, a little slower to rev. The smart convertible was an old friend, and always in for a fight.

Out of habit she'd put an attractive, pearl-handled pooshka in the glove compartment, along with a tool set, a small bottle of narcotikes disguised in an empty bottle of her kindly housekeeper Mrs. Gruen's smelling salts, an extra pair of clean white perchatkas just in case she'd need to nicen up her appearance for polite company or conceal her prints in a hurry.

In rehab they had given young Ms. Droog a diploma, detailing her Upstanding Accomplishments. She wrapped this now around a stick of TNT, secured the tight tube of paper with a spare hair elastic (always prepared was Nancy) and lit the fuse end off her cigarillo. She conducted a last crescendo with her explosive wand before flinging it into an orchard of fruit trees to go BOOM seconds later.

She smoked, patted her head scarf and laughed.

"Muzyka!" she yelled into the night.

With notes crashing around her and the wind in her normally neat blonde hair she planned to viddy her old stomping grounds, the nameless saloons where they'd planned and the scenes of her grimiest crimes so to speak, dear reader, and decide where she'd go from here on out now that the doctors promised her dear respectable father that they had fixed her naughty old mind up right.

It was good to be back in the old driver's seat, she was anxious to rejoin her friends. Young Miss Droog took matters of justice into her own manicured, horrorshow hands, this was going to be a dynamite evening.

My Son Takes an Interest

Meredith Counts

I glare at my son, Sammy, who had to tag along with me to my doctor's appointment and is chewing on a folded-up drinking straw. It's his new habit, clacking it so loudly that I wondered how hard it would be to adopt him out, before full-blown puberty hits, before I die of exhaustion. At least he's not smoking, is what his dad says. He's eleven. My son, not my husband. Sammy's with me because he's suspended from school. He's suspended from school for cussing and fighting. We're here because I'm sick as a dog. I'm so congested that the noise seems to get trapped in there, echoing through the congestion. About to tell him to throw the straw away, I'm distracted when the moaning starts in the room next to us.

Like, really loud moaning. WHAAAA OOOOOOOOH the man in the room next to us is going, WHAAA OOOO NNNNNNNNGNNNN OOOOOOOH. Loud enough to make us catch each other's eyes. My son's eyes are laughing, his mouth hangs open and the straw wad in there rattles for a second then rests, unchewed.

Sammy was suspended after telling another sixth-grader to fuck himself during a shoving match that started when the other kid teased him with a life-sized Friendship Mannequin and Sam tackled both the kid and the doll. He actually told the other kid to "fuck yourself with an alternating current," which is sort of brilliant, and a result of Sam being on an inventors kick, but this sort of thing doesn't seem to be helping him to make friends who will help him survive middle school.

Then in a break in the moaning we hear the door click shut next door and the nurses start talking in the hallway.

"His ears are just jammed with wax, just full of it."

At least three voices discuss who is going to flush the loud moaner's ears.

Fascinated, Sam shushes me. I haven't made a peep.

One says it's gross, so gross.

They don't know we can hear them.

Another says this kind of thing is "honestly not that gross. Cysts are gross . . ."

"Oh, wait 'til you see," the first one says.

Sammy is thrilled. He's beaming. I have to laugh. This is the kid who never hesitated to grab a fish to remove a hook. He squirms in discomfort when people kiss on television, but that's different.

The moaning starts up again.

My entire life, I've been encouraged to be quiet, quieter, an invisible helper, make it look effortless, don't make a scene, and here this man is just moaning, moaning aloud, moaning to fill the entire building with the sound of himself of his own discomfort.

Presumably someone is handing over supplies, and we hear them say, in a cheery, teasing voice: "Here you go, girl, get him to sign the forms and go to town!"

"Gross!" Sam hisses.

Honestly, I haven't seen him this engaged in anything for months.

When we hear the door click and she goes in to get the man's signature, his moaning increases in volume and intensity. There's a blood pressure thing mounted to the wall between us, and the moaning is loud enough to make the cords tremble.

"He's only moaning because she has to listen," I say.

Sammy shushes me.

We hear the water running over there. Sam's eyes widen. It is a loud, forceful whooshing. It sounds like they're cleaning this person's head with a garden hose.

"Which ear do you want me to do first?" she asks.

"Are you having as much fun as I am?" he asks her in a flirty voice.

Sam and I jerk our heads to look at each other, both of our faces saying "What!? No!"

She pauses for a really long time.

"It's been a really crazy morning," she says, finally.

"Now you lay very still and I will be back in to check on you in fifteen minutes to see if we're breaking this up for you."

When the doctor comes in for me, she starts to speak and is interrupted by the moans of the man next door.

"Wow, you can really hear everything in here," she says.

As we talk she diagnoses me with a sinus infection, I am given a prescription, but my ailments take a backseat as all three of us listen to the moaning man.

There is a clatter next door, and the sound of the running water changes, the man yelps "shit!" and then "nurse! nurse!"

"He's knocked the sprayer loose," the doctor says.

"He's really loud," my son says.

Both of us adults look at Sammy, and then we all laugh. Even though I am pissed at this kid for getting expelled, it's good to see him smiling. It's great to see him interacting with another adult in a totally normal way, it's so great to see him quietly smiling after making a stranger laugh.

"How do I say this without violating any privacy laws," she says. "Okay, when a patient has a large amount of wax in both ears, they often can't hear, it affects the hearing."

We hear a nurse come in to rescue the man. "Oh God, you're soaked," she tells him.

While my doctor is filling out a form on her tablet, Sammy asks how long it takes to clear out someone's ears.

"Oh, quite a while."

I look down at Sammy's shoe, his leg is hitched up and crossed so that one ankle rests on the other knee. He's fretting with the elastic on his sock because he's excited, and I see that there is writing in pen on his leg. Normally it would be covered by his pantleg; he has written something there that he doesn't want anyone to see.

We settle up and walk out. Now Sammy sidles up close to me and asks in a low voice if we can stay to see this guy once he's done.

All I want in this world is to get my drugs and go home to my bed, but I can feel the constant annoyance part of parenting slip away and I remember the joy of giving this kid something he wants.

My happy baby is growing up and he doesn't want to do sports. He quit karate. He used to love cooking and baking and now he says he hates it. Getting him to do homework and put away his laundry is an ordeal. But here is something he wants to do. He has taken an interest in something: he wants to spy on the unbelievably loud old man with jammed ears.

Now, yes, this is gross. But I am supposed to support his interests. I've read so in all the articles. I don't think it's illegal to get a look at someone who has put on such a public performance.

I lean over and whisper to my son. I can't remember the last time he let me get that close. I don't care that his winter coat smells like a hamster cage. I don't even mind when I hear his teeth clacking on the straw.

He smiles and nods. We laugh like conspirators.

There is a drive-thru pharmacy I've used before that's next to a McDonalds near here.

We drop off my script, we pick up flavored coffee drinks and cheeseburgers. If I can't climb into bed, then I'll have caffeine with whipped cream on top with my weird son. Then I drive us back to the parking lot of the doctor's office, and we stake it out, eating, drinking our coffees while I wait for my prescription to be filled and my son theorizes about which car belongs to the man we'd overheard moaning in there.

"He's going to be all wet," Sammy laughs in anticipation.

He unwraps his second cheeseburger. The coffee is so sweet that it's making him happy; it's coffee enough that it will get me through the afternoon.

The radio is off and the heat is on. A figure appears in the doorway of the doctor's office and we go high alert, then we see it is an old woman and we relax. I'm not going to ask him about the fight at school for the tenth time. I relax enough that I don't need to rehash all that. We're cozy here with our junk food, spying like creeps on somebody's old guy with a health problem. But we're spying like creeps as a family.

Gulf

Michael Williamson

Jerome can't think of children without thinking of eels. A whole skein of them, coiled around the end of his father's fishing hook twenty years ago, when Jerome was ten years old. They'd spent the afternoon together on the Mississippi coast of the Gulf of Mexico, through which they shored in his father's speedboat only to anchor and sit in the sun, the only sound between them the white noise hum of waves. By the time his father caught the eels, Jerome had already learned that nothing good could come from the water, though he screamed at the sight of their wiggly bodies anyway, and shrank only after he caught his father's scowl. "Don't be such a pussy," his father said, and with two cool steps, leaned forward to snip the line, after which the eels splashed back below the surface and drenched Jerome's sneakers with a cataract of water.

With his forearm, Jerome's father peeled a layer of sweat from his forehead. His shirt was off, crumpled in a corner of the boat, and even then Jerome could see the similarities in their bodies. "Like looking into a goddamn mirror," his father would always say. A cruel thing to say, but he wasn't wrong. Jerome would have been a fool to deny that from him he'd inherited that knotty, bird-narrow frame. Only seventeen years older than him, Jerome's father's body was still unmarked by age or overuse, his lanky arms and legs afflicted with the same bulbous joints he'd passed on to his son.

Jerome's father peered over the edge of the boat and spat out a cud of tar-colored saliva, which floated on the surface of the water. "There's supposed to be a cove here where groupers like to scurry off to. I seen it on the map." He pouted at Jerome as if for approval, a look at which

Jerome could only nod. "We're staying out here, damn it, till I catch at least one of these grouper ass sons of bitches."

Jerome too peered over the gunwale. The water was not the blue of California postcards, but brackish and ugly, the sort of place it made sense you'd pull eels from. Jerome couldn't fathom how, if the water contained something so ugly as eels, it might also contain anything his father might want to bring home.

For the rest of the day, his father's wish for grouper continued to evade him. Instead, he reeled in an assortment of oddities: infant silky sharks, wire-mustached toadfish, luminous hakes glistening in their oily translucence. Each unwanted catch stoked his anger, and Jerome, already given enough reason to fear these bouts of rage, soon found that he couldn't scoot further away from his father without jumping into the water. All the while, Jerome's line remained unbitten. He was done up in a bright orange life vest, a confusion of plush rectangles with nylon cords pulled tight. Even over his skinny body, it was tight, and sweat dribbled down his forehead and off the tip of his sunburnt nose. He hated fishing.

Still, he reeled his line in from time to time anyway. Once in a while he secured a new worm to the hook at its end just to pass the time, though he hoped nothing would take it. The sun by that point had turned pink, and cast its glow on mud-brown water that refused to reflect it. His father, from the opposite end of the boat, mumbled a spree of swear words, his eyes on the bobber floating a few yards ahead.

When at first it happened, Jerome almost didn't notice. It was only the slightest of tugs, after all, faint enough it might have been a tug of the wind. Besides, he didn't know thing one about fishing. The second pull, a strong yank that just about shirked the rod from his hands, was unmistakable and rocketed Jerome to his feet. With nowhere else to turn, he locked eyes with his father. His heart bobbed under his life vest, and his shaky wrists made his rod tremble.

"Reel in the goddamn thing," his father said. "Only you better not catch no grouper before I do."

Jerome hardly heard his father over the pulses of blood in his ears, but still he hunkered his shoulders and reeled. The tip of his rod bent to its outermost pliancy, and Jerome was sure he would be pulled into the gulf along with it. A flame of pain sparked in his elbows and spread like wildfire into his shoulders and wrists. His line danced on the surface of the water, patterned with the hectic motions of the life that struggled underneath. With one final pull, and a briny throng of water, his catch breached the surface. The force of its exit knocked him backward and, as he fell, a kitelike shadow tumbled through his vision. Before he saw anything else, he heard the flop of a fish, his father swearing. When he turned, he let out his second scream of the day, and scooted away in terror. There it was, his catch: an angry-tailed stingray bustled against the boat floor. Seawater wicked a diamond of wetness into the bristly boat carpet around it.

The stingray was the dull gray of a morning shadow, but slimy and coruscating. About the size of a baseball plate, its paper-thin body rippled and revolted on the floor. It offered in its movements a peek of its underbelly, where its gills worked to breathe delicious water and then heaved with repulsion at the intake of air. A hillock of flesh mohawked down its middle, two probing black eyes stuck on either side. Jerome felt the adrenaline of fear stream through him, menaced as he was by the thing's presence, and yet he couldn't, despite his best efforts, make himself look away. More than anything, he wanted the thing dunked back underwater, as far from him as he could make it.

His father stomped through the boat and cut the line from the pole. He moved to grab at the stingray, but retracted his hand when its stinger curled upward. From a compartment in the floor of the boat, he grabbed a long, silver-handled fishing net and, using its butt end, prodded the stingray. In response, it flapped its pectoral fins as though slapping away a nuisance, and sloshed itself against the carpet in an angry, fleshy racket. Jerome's father, with one hand woven into the net's mesh, growled and attempted once more to push the fish up and over the gunwale, but sneered as he watched it sag downward. It landed back on the carpet in a glop, its stinger pointed skyward.

He stomped a foot near the stingray. "Get out of my boat, you son of a bitch," he said, a vague threat the stingray met with a swish of its arm-length tail, which skimmed the outsole of his boot. His face florid above his narrow, sunburned torso, Jerome's father turned the fishing net over in his palms to grasp it by the handle. He turned the loop of it sideways above his head and then whapped the stingray first once, then twice, then endlessly in a thwacking staccato. Defenseless, the stingray writhed and rippled its slatted gills in glissandos of pain. Flecks of blood spattered Jerome's face and life vest and still his father didn't cease banging the net against the animal till the strikes became clunky, at which point he had pierced through its body and hammered the boat floor. Even the boat picked up his angry inertia. It careened on the water, and knotted Jerome's stomach in seasickness.

Violent as it was, the scene captivated Jerome, enthralled him. He had wanted the stingray gone, after all, and there his father was, granting his wish. He'd never seen his father's violence from this perspective—always on the receiving end before—and to see it now frightened him, yes, but not in any of the ways he might have expected. Under the sun, each freckly tendon and familiar protuberance of his father's lanky frame shone. Like looking into a goddamn mirror. If their bodies, Jerome realized, were unified in shape, in silhouette, so too must they be unified in utility. That's what frightened him most when, covered in a strange cocktail of blood, sweat, and seawater, his father tossed aside the bloodied net. Still in a heap on the boat floor, Jerome expected to feel revulsion; but when he laid eyes on the stingray's corpse—unrecognizable from its dozens of dents, folded over like dirty laundry—he felt only a sense of relief at it being gone. As Jerome took the sight in, his father kicked the stingray overboard and let out a loud whoop, his teeth bared for the first time all day. The sun pouring into his eyes, Jerome watched his father's reaction. And as he did, it occurred to him, with dam-bursting immediacy, what uncanny tricks genetics will play on you. His father turned to him, his cheeks curled up into a grin, and when, by accident, their eyes met, Jerome could feel the distinct pressure of shame wobble in his joints.

Over the months and years that followed, that shame stuck with him, and charted a course for the onset of his maturity. Under its guidance, he felt his posture recede to conceal his height, heard his voice fade to a near whisper, felt all his buds of anger wither over time. And when, as a grown-up, he watched his father die under the fluorescent-bulb sting of a hospital room, as a ventilator sighed his final breaths into his lungs, Jerome could think only of the stingray. It was the second time in his life he'd felt glad to see something go. Under the ratty hospital blanket, with skin jaundiced and sunken from illness, his father's body had never seemed knobbier—like a series of knots tied into a strand of rope. Jerome recognized the familiar odd angles of his ankles, the forward lean of his generous shoulders, those clunky, unattractive knees—all the things he'd spent so long inside himself trying to transform into meaningless, conjunctive nonsense.

Jerome can't bring himself to share any of this with his husband, Garrett. The last time he did—two months ago now, back when Garrett first started begging to adopt a child—Garrett responded with, "I still think you'd be a wonderful father." And then, he had pulled Jerome into a kiss and said, "You're a different sort of person than all that."

And that's just the thing, isn't it? Though it would pain Garrett to hear it, Jerome is more confident of what he has become than he's ever let on, more aware of his most private self than he could ever express. Even in that moment, Jerome had kissed his husband back, though he sensed, just beneath the surface of their calm, a current of anger work its way through his chest. Garrett was wrong about him, and the desire to say so bubbled up near Jerome's voice. But he had learned by then when to keep quiet, when it was better to follow his husband's lead.

Right now, Garrett snores in bed beside him. For the second time this week, he's fallen asleep reading a pamphlet from an adoption agency, which lies tented open on his chest. On its cover are pictures of toothy, multiracial families. Men and women cavort with happy children beneath words in a tacky font reading "START YOUR FAMILY TODAY!" When Jerome turns to look at his sleeping partner, all these memories of his father are made to dissolve like salt in his throat. He thumps the pamphlet and watches as it sails to the carpet with a papery *splat*. He thinks of what he might say the next time Garrett feels brave enough to broach the subject of children. Probably nothing, he is sure. But his silence will do nothing to change his mind. He can't stand breaking Garrett's heart, but he knows he doesn't want children, knows he wants to snip his father's influence where he can. He has never been surer of anything in his life.

He has become, though, so prone to capitulation.

Lit by dull, lemon-yellow lamplight, Jerome turns away from Garrett and secures himself beneath the covers. The thought occurs to him—frightening and real—that there's a chance if he continues to stay silent and Garrett keeps pushing, what he wants might wash away over time.

Who knows—maybe the friction of their efforts will spark into something Jerome never saw coming, and they will adopt Garrett's children: little Caleb and Puloma. Painful as it is, it isn't so hard to imagine. Together, they could devise their own tenets of fatherhood. They will swing piñatas from oak branches on birthdays and bronze baby shoes as totems for the mantle. When the children discover new and visionary ways to hurt him, disappoint him, anger him, Jerome will wait for Garrett to come guide him through the difficult process of learning to love them. One day, while the children are still young, they might even take them to the aquarium. Followed by pinballing shoals of fish, Garrett and Jerome will push them along in their joint stroller through the arching, glass-covered hallways, their interlocked hands dangling between them. As a family, they'll stare open-mouthed at tanks of pink jellyfish waltzing through spumes of water. When no one else is looking, Jerome might let the children tickle the flesh of a skate in a shallow pool, and delight as they recoil at its unexpected viscosity. And when the kids get tired and doze into naps, and Garrett is ready to go home, Jerome will ask forgiveness as he disbands from the group, as he pauses to look up at the expansive bands of brick-thick glass and marvels at all that inaccessible life laid bare before his eyes, squeezing past one another in disjointed, circular harmony—octopus, sturgeon, pipefish, barracuda.

Villians Or I Dream in Science Fiction

Shawn Shiflett

I'm on a planet that is inhabited by three humanoid species. My species is called the "Villains." I'm sure that long ago we had a more befitting name for our proud people, but centuries of warring with the other two species has left us worn down into accepting their nickname for us. The tide of battle has long since turned hopeless, and now we are on the verge of extinction, the last fifteen of us piling rocks in our quarry to be used for defensive walls. We are as thin as celluloid film, opaquely black with a plastic sheen, and no more detailed than block cutout figures lacking hands, feet or even facial features on our square heads. In fact, one of us is completely indistinguishable from the next, but far from looking at our lack of physical individuality as a handicap, it is a source of unity among us. Our leader stands high up on a rock pile and exhorts us to "Keep working! Villains deserve to live, too!" He has one of those deep, gravelly voices known to baddies the cosmos over. The walls that we have painstakingly built across our lands have failed to protect us from our enemies, as their well-trained soldiers are adept at tunneling under or climbing over our rocky defenses with the stealth of big cats. Out running them is impossible as both enemy species can cover over ten feet with a single bound. And because they always attack under the cover of night, we catch only the moonlit glint of a saber, the silhouette of a bulky frame, or an occasional skeletal hand that hangs ape-like lower than a soldier's knees. We've never really been able to differentiate between their species, for they share a common language of snarls and grunts leading many to hypothesize that they are close species cousins.

Each day, we Villains keep methodically working, determined to cling to our rock-piling culture and to keep building our walls even higher, though high enough has always proven beyond reach. Soon night will fall, and we will be hunted again. Cave-dwelling hideouts are no match for our cunning adversaries' coordinated attack. Then at daybreak, after they retreat again dragging the corpses of our slaughtered comrades as trophies, those of us lucky enough to have survived will return to the quarry to work once again. Gathering rocks when you don't have any hands is the hardest of hard labor.

White Dove

Shawn Shiflett

I'm teeing off at a golf course. Despite my not ever having played the game, my swing is textbook perfect, and I drive the ball far and high over the fairway, sand traps, trees, and ponds. I'm admiring its straight-as-an-archer's arrow trajectory, when it meets a flock of white doves, turns into one of them, and soars away.

Napalm Déjà vu

Shawn Shiflett

I'm leading a squad of soldiers across a meadow that's boxed in on all sides by tall apartment buildings. Each of us is slowly sweeping his rifle from side to side as we wade through waist high grass, in search of hidden enemy. Someone yells, "Napalm!" and we hit the ground, only to be in the oncoming path of a fireball that billows, rolls, and consume us. The skin on my arms is curdling off of raw muscle, and surely my nervous system is on the brink of reacting with excruciating pain. Then a booming voice—whether from a P.A. system or God himself—announces, "DO OVER."

Once again, I'm leading a squad of soldiers across a meadow that's boxed in on all sides by tall apartment buildings. Each of us is slowly sweeping his rifle from side to side as we wade through waist high grass, in search of hidden enemy. Someone yells, "Napalm!" I look up at the clear blue sky and see a flying machine that reminds me of a lunar lander, its spidery legs covered in electronic gadgets. It glides toward a soft landing on a building's flat rooftop, bounces on the tarred black surface from one footpad to another, only to then crash against a chimney. The impact knocks a couple of the lander's hoses loose, and they begin to spew liquid napalm. I'm no dummy, and before so much as a spark can ignite a second inferno, I throw down my rifle and take off running across the meadow. From behind me, I hear the boom and whoosh of an explosion, followed by the sickening screams of my men who are engulfed in flames, but I've already reached a gangway and start scrambling down cement steps. They lead to a basement that's lit only by a shaft of sunlight coming through a narrow, screened window high on the far wall. It looks out onto a peaceful residential side street lined with shady trees, exactly where I want to be. There's no time to waste, and I launch myself, leading with my feet as I catapult across the room, hoping that I can kick out the screen and then skip like a stone across a pond into a safe world beyond. But the closer I get to the window, the more I can see that the screen is made of heavy-duty wires, and my escape is far from certain.

The Next Chapter

Rebecca McClanahan

Late October leaves spiral down from the willow oaks as I drive cautiously behind Dad's Buick. I still think of the Buick as Dad's, though he is one year dead. And I still think of Mother as his wife, though she has no memory of their seventy-two years together. Last week she asked me if she was old enough to have children yet.

In the driver's seat of the Buick is my sister Claudia. Beside her, Mother is so small that I can see only the top of her head. When we left Claudia's house a few minutes ago, I strapped the seat belt around Mother and kissed her cheeks, one then the other, as if sending a child on a long journey. In fact, our destination is only a few miles away: the modest house set deep in the pines, where a dark-haired woman and her husband wait for us. We have brought Mother to the house three times now. "Baby steps" is how I think of the Sunday visits. Rehearsals for a day I'd hoped would never come. "What is your mother's favorite color?" the woman asked me last week. Her Romanian accent is strong, and I had to listen with my eyes as well as my ears. I told her that baby blue would go well with Mother's quilt. "Good, we like blue," she answered, adding that her husband would get right on it; he wanted the bedroom paint to be dry when Mother arrived.

"Precious cargo," I whispered to Claudia as I closed the passenger door on the Buick. Claudia nodded, her beautiful face wet with tears. Of the four daughters, she alone inherited Mother's distinctive, wide-set eyes and arched brows. We'd decided earlier that Mother, our most precious cargo, should ride in the spacious, leather-seated Buick. I would follow behind in my Toyota, its backseat packed with what is left of Mother's "earthly possessions," as my parents' minister called the things that crowd out our lives. Little is left to crowd out Mother's: four boxes of clothes, one quilt that Claudia and I chose from the dozens our mother once stitched, a carton of puzzles and crayons to keep Mother's hands busy, and a stack of books spanning her perennial girlhood: fairy tales, nursery rhymes, *Black Beauty, Anne of Green Gables.* Endings escape Mother; her mind can hold only a few pages at a time. So each time I read from the book, Mother worries aloud about Anne, the red-haired orphan. "I hope they keep her," she always says, of the aging couple who hesitate to take Anne in.

We pass a horse pasture circled with a white fence. North Carolina autumns can be breathtaking, especially along winding country roads like this one. I'm glad Claudia is taking the curves slowly. I wish the drive could last longer. Now Mother turns toward Claudia, probably to ask something. Maybe she thinks we're finally taking her back to Indiana. "It's getting late," she says each evening when the sky begins to darken. She has been saying this for four years, ever since we moved her and Dad to North Carolina so we could care for them here. "Time to go home now," she always repeats. "My parents will be wondering where I am."

Or maybe, on this brilliant October morning, Mother understands exactly where we are taking her. Such flashes of clarity happen when we least expect them, recognition sparking in her eyes: Suddenly, we are not strangers, we are her daughters, and her sons are her sons. I once longed for this. To be *known* again! To have my mother back! But recognition always comes with a price, the sting of loss that appears visibly on her face: Her parents are gone, her sister and brothers, her husband, her home. In these moments, too, Mother recognizes herself, naming what she sees: An old woman who is no use anymore. A burden to her children. "Be careful," she always says when she reaches for an arm to steady her. "Be careful I don't take you down with me."

"Never happen," I joke, working to lighten such moments. The truth is, the years of caregiving took me down more times than I can count. I'd planned to care for them both until the end, never imagining how difficult it would be. Beyond the unending tasks and the constant medical emergencies, there were Dad's night terrors and Mother's delusions and wanderings. The day after Dad's funeral, I finally confessed to my siblings that I couldn't do it anymore. Yes, *confessed* is the word I need here. A public airing of a private shame. And *relief*, the feeling that followed: Claudia would take Mother. My life would be mine again. *Mine*: another word I'd lost track of years before. The cry of a child, grabbing what she claims as her own. Her own and no one else's.

But what of my sister's life? With each day I have gained this past year, Claudia has lost one of her own. And now, she has been taken down too. "It's okay, Sis," I said this morning as we carried the last box from Mother's bedroom, which Claudia had furnished with such bright hope. "We can still see her each week."

Claudia looked up, her eyes wild with pain. She did not want to do this.

"It's been a year," I reminded her, as if either of us needed reminding. "You've done all you can, let it go." I was thinking of the Alice Munro story I read last night, its wisdom and hard-edged love. In the story, a mother recalls a time when her young daughter's life was in peril, and as I read I imagined the two characters drawing closer, touching each other tenderly—isn't that the way such things go? But no, the story mother confesses that when she touched her daughter, she was careful "not to feel anything much." The "forms of love," she now saw, could include a love "measured and disciplined, because you have to survive."

Mother turns her face back to the window, pointing to something in the distance. Does she recognize this curving road, the red barn, the horse stables we are now passing? In a few minutes, when we reach our destination, will she remember the pine trees and the house? "Maybe they'll want to keep me," Mother said last week as I drove her back to Claudia's after a visit with the woman. There was no lightness in her voice, no hopeful longing. It was a statement, flatly simple. Recalling it now, my mind seizes. Was she trying to tell me that she understands? That she knows what the next chapter holds? I imagine the woman dressing Mother for bed, buttoning the pink flowered gown I gave her years ago. Tucking her in. Leaving the nightlight on in case Mother calls out, as she often does—for her mother, her father. When I was a child and a shadow startled me, Mother always came when I called, kneeling beside my bed and stroking my hair until I fell into sleep.

Today is Saturday, so maybe the woman's grandchildren will be there, too, as they are most weekends, crowding the fragrant, steamy kitchen with their shrieks and sweet bluster—and kisses for their ancient visitor. Scroll back sixty years and it might be our family kitchen, the dark-haired woman at the stove our own mother. Except she isn't. The woman is a fairy-tale version of our mother. Warm and kind, yes, but a stranger from a foreign land, her accent marking the distances she has traveled to arrive in this country, where work is plentiful. This strange country, where daughters leave their mothers.

We pass another pasture, where spotted horses graze. The houses grow smaller; a few trailers appear. Now here comes a white church, and another. The childhood rhyme comes to me—"Here is the church, here is the steeple"—and our young, beautiful Mother showing us how to fold and unfold our small hands to "open the door and see all the people!" Does Mother sense that this will be her new family? How can we bear to do this?

Yet we are. Look at us bearing it. Bearing our little mother away. Ahead, the Buick's turn signal flashes. The stand of pine trees thickens, then clears: Here is the house. Here is the porch. Here is the kind, dark-haired woman, waiting by the door to receive us.

Five Stories about Kenny George: An Apology for Professor X

billy lombardo

I've been holding onto this letter for a long time. I started writing it in the fall of 2007 when I worried that you might return to teach for the winter term of the low-res MFA program at ___ ___ College.

One of the Book Talk classes we could choose to attend during that residency was *Nine Stories,* and I had a feeling you might be teaching it. So, I put a number 1 by the *Nine Stories* option, and I got accepted! I figured if you ended up being the teacher, I was going to face the music.

I had a lot of questions about *Nine Stories.* Like how did J.D. get away with all that POV business in *Down at the Dinghy*? I had questions about *Bananafish,* too; I'm pretty sure I got the point—Seymour's torment and all that—but, wow.

I don't remember much about the other seven stories. *Franny & Zooey* is fresher. That bathroom scene with Zooey and Bessie—Jesus, that's tough to read. He calls her a fat old druid, and tells her I don't know how many times to get the hell out of the bathroom so he can finish his goddam ablutions in peace. He gets so angry at her at when she says Lane told her that Franny got that little green book out of the library and not off Seymour's desk where the book had been I don't know how many goddam years. Zooey says it's *depressing*, but it's something else. But then Bessie says, "I don't go in that room if I can help it, and you know it." She says, "I don't look at Seymour's old—at his things."

Zooey isn't finished being awful to Bessie, but when she says that about Seymour's *things* there's a little shift. He finally reels it back a little. He's been a dick to her for like two hours, and he finally says, "All right, I'm sorry."

In your Book Talk did you, like, draw a pile of all the examples of him being a dick to her on the white board and then stack it against that apology?

Anyway, I don't know if you knew this, but after I applied to the MFA program I got a letter saying I wasn't accepted, and I don't know if I even cared, then—I sort of expected it—but the next day, the director called me and said it was a mistake. I was in! It was a clerical error, he said, and I was like, *no problem, everyone makes mistakes.* I was accepted!

The whole low residency program was a little tricky, because 1) I never thought I'd get accepted in the first place, and 2) my wife wasn't crazy about me going back to school because of the five ten-day residencies I would have to take for the program, and 3) the winter residencies always cut into the academic year at the Latin School of Chicago where I taught.

And that first residency was going to be especially tricky because my son was in summer school for algebra, and if he didn't get at least a B— they weren't going to let him go to Nazareth Academy, and *I* was the one who helped him with homework.

I was still pretty excited about getting into the MFA program, but when I got there they put me in a workshop with all of these very smart people who used words like *polysyndeton,* as in, *Nice use of polysyndeton, there!* and I would look at my friend Matthew and make a crazy questioning face and mouth the question, *Polysyndeton? Is that even a word?* And he would close his eyes and nod sadly that it was most definitely a word, and I started thinking that the real mistake wasn't the rejection letter—it was the acceptance phone call.

Do you remember that piece you read at the faculty reading that first residency when I met you? It was about your old man. It was nice how you read it, too, even though I guess you stuttered a little. I didn't know who you were or anything, but I was thinking maybe when I got back to Chicago I would email you to see if you might give me a blurb for a book I had coming out that year.

I didn't even know your last name. And also, there were two other teachers with the same first name. One was a black dude, but the other one, he was also white, and also bald. He borrowed someone's guitar one night and played a bunch of Paul Simon tunes. But it wasn't enough to help me remember his last name, so when I emailed one of my classmates to ask her if she knew which one of you was the one I was thinking of, I had to describe you. Isn't that what everyone does?

So, I said, *Hey (friend), who was that old, bald, stuttering guy whose first name is_____? He read that piece about his old man? Not the guy who was playing Paul Simon songs that night. The other one.*

So, my friend told me you were _____ _____, and she gave me your email address. All I had to do was select it and copy it and paste it right back in the *To* line.

I rubbed my hands together like I was getting ready to do something big, and I set the cursor there at the top of that email and pushed all the words of the old email down and got to business.

I wish I still had the paragraph I wrote to you, about how I admired your writing, and the range of emotions in that piece and all that. It was a pretty good paragraph.

And how fast did you respond? Jesus. Back then I would keep checking my email every minute if I was home, but I'm not sure I was home. Maybe I was picking up my son, Kane, from basketball practice or something. He was a freshman in high school by then. Oh, boy. That's another story.

He ended up with a C— in that algebra class he took. My wife got pissed at me all over again because I chose to get an MFA instead of helping him with his summer school algebra homework that summer, which is pretty ironic (if I'm even using that word right) because that's the class I had to go to summer school for when I was a kid, too.

So, I called the nun who was the Dean of Academics at the school and told her I was a teacher and I knew about kids and Kane was a good kid and he deserved a chance and our only other option was this public school that was not going to be a good fit at all for him—it was going to be terrible—but this nun was a piece of work. She wouldn't budge. *He should have thought about that before he got a C—,* she said.

So, I wrote a letter to the baseball coach because he knew a little bit about Kane playing baseball, and I wrote a letter to the president of the school about how great a kid my son is. And I had Kane's eighth-grade teachers write letters about his character, and then the admissions director called us in for a meeting, either to tell us that Kane was in or Kane was out—I didn't know which—and I took Kane there with me, and the admissions director, who was also the basketball coach, looked at Kane and he pointed on his fingers all the things I did to help Kane get into Nazareth, and then he said the rest was up to Kane. They were going to let him in! Oh, I wish I could describe to you how happy we were when the guy looked across the table at and said, *Welcome to Nazareth, Kane!* Just thinking about it now, I'm starting to cry a little bit.

It was later that same year—in December, I think—that we heard what happened to Kenny George. Did you know Kenny George? I won't be surprised if you heard about him. He played basketball for UNC at Asheville—tallest person to ever play NCAA basketball. Seven feet seven inches!

Back when I taught him in high school, though, he was barely seven-one. Kane was in maybe the third grade at The Latin School, same place where I taught Kenny in high school, and one day I picked Kane up from the lower school, and I brought him to my office and we went into the gym, and lo and behold! who was shooting hoops all by himself on the roof gym? Kenny George! You should have seen Kane's face. It was the first time he ever saw Kenny up close. He didn't even come up to Kenny's belt!

Kenny put his hand way down by Kane's head and gave him a low-five and Kane gave Kenny a high-five. Then Kenny had some fun with Kane. He passed the basketball to him and then went under the basket and stood there flat footed and every time Kane took a shot Kenny put his giant hand up and caught the ball. Every time. Every time Kane just looked at me like *did you see what just happened*? That basketball was like a little cantaloupe in Kenny's hand.

Kenny wasn't too good at moving around. He always came to classes late because his body didn't work like the rest of ours. He didn't get around so gracefully.

One time I was sitting on the stage in the auditorium waiting to make an announcement, and I looked in the back of the theater and there was Kenny by the theater door; it was propped open with a stopper and Kenny stood there resting his chin on his hands on the top of the door! That's how tall he was!

Anyway, that winter of Kane's freshman year at Nazareth, I picked him up from basketball practice one day in December, and we went to Johnnie's Beef in Elmwood Park. We had the radio on in the Nissan. Kane was struggling in school, and that's what we were talking about. That's almost all we talked about. He was angry at how easy it was for his friends and how hard it was for him, and he said he didn't think he was ever going to graduate. One time, we were in Chipotle in Oak Park and Kane told me that. He said, "I don't know how I'm ever going to get through high school, Dad."

But that night at Johnnies Beef, all of a sudden Kane remembered what his basketball coach told him about Kenny George.

Oh, I almost forgot, he said. Coach Bonk told me to tell you what happened to Kenny George.

Every coach in Chicago knew Kenny George. And Coach Bonk knew I had taught Kenny, so the coach told Kane to tell me that Kenny had part of his foot amputated.

I was holding my beef sandwich up, and it was dripping onto the waxed wrapper on my lap. The Nissan was a new car then. Kane would smash it up on New Year's Eve a couple of years later. He wouldn't get hurt, though.

So, Kane told me about Kenny's foot, then, but only like he was relaying a message; I'm not sure he understood. I was holding the last part of my beef sandwich there and Kane paused in his anger just long enough to tell me about Kenny's foot, and I guess I just stopped eating.

I thought about a story a kid told me about when Kenny's high school coach made one of his point guards run suicides wearing Kenny's shoes, because the kid was making fun of how slow Kenny was. I guess Kenny used to get his shoes from Shaquille O'Neal when Shaq was done with them, and when Kenny's feet got too big he had to keep wearing Shaq's shoes, because I guess no one made shoes that big. His feet were always bleeding.

So, there we were at Johnnie's, Kane and me—worried about algebra and Spanish and religion—while Kenny was lying in a giant's bed somewhere with half a foot, and I just kept saying *Fuck*. One second we were eating beefs and the next second I was swearing and the next second we were both of us crying.

Anyway, that day at Johnnie's was around the same time I asked you for a blurb for that little book I had coming out. I want to say it was only about fifteen minutes after I hit the send button on that email when I got a reply from you. This is what you said:

Old, bald, stuttering guy. Let me get this straight. You want a blurb?

I scrolled down to see all I wrote in that original email, but you had deleted it. I was going to go back to my Send box to find it but when I saw it sitting there I don't think I even read it. I didn't want to see it anymore, so I deleted it. I wanted to delete everything I ever did on a computer.

I wrote another email to you right after that, too. I can imagine what I wrote. I know how I get when I do shit like that; I say things like, *I'm a dick. I'm just a dick sometimes, and I don't think. My problem is sometimes I want to make people laugh, but I'm not mean.*

Listen to this other thing I did once—this proves what I dick I am. It was me and a group of us from Bridgeport, I don't know who all was with us, but we were like five or eight of us there—all about sixteen or eighteen years old—and we were at Oak Street Beach, and there was a bunch of black dudes sitting on those giant cement steps, and one of them asked if we wanted to buy weed, and one of us said, No. Then the black dude said, What's wrong, you don' t like weed?

I can't even tell you what I said. I don't think I'll ever tell anyone what I said. It was another thing I said that I wish I could forget. There's a lot of things like that. But I said it. I most certainly said it.

And the big dude picked up a bottle—looking at me the whole time—and he cracked it on one of those cement steps like in a movie, and he came at me with it.

That's what it took for me to realize what I had done. A broken beer bottle coming at me like that.

I never thought I'd tell that story to anyone.

Anyway, after I wrote whatever I wrote in that email, in the way of an apology to you, there was something like a hot wet washrag around my heart. It was almost as hot as the water gets straight from the faucet. I make bread on Sundays and for the yeast to rise it has to be in this little window of temperature between 105° and 115°. The washrag was a little hotter than that. That's pretty hot for an exposed heart.

I kept checking my email every minute to see if you had responded to my apology, but there was nothing. You never responded.

So, my second residency was that winter after we found out about Kenny George's foot. You weren't at that residency, and I was like, *phew.* Same with my third residency that next July. And then the fourth one came, which is when I signed up for the *Nine Stories* Book Talk and I got in it and read the stories right away. But then I got an email from the program administrator who said, *There's a problem. Call me.*

I was like, *Oh, shit. _____ _____ is going to be there.* I just knew it. You didn't want me in the *Nine Stories* Book Talk because it was going to be awkward. The program administrator felt bad for me when I told her the story, and then she put me in another Book Talk and I had to read a war book I can't remember for shit.

My classmate who emailed me your name felt bad for me, too, but she was like, Anyway, Famous Actor is going to be there, and that's all anyone is going to be talking about.

And I said: Who's Famous Actor, and she told me a couple of films Famous Actor was in, and none of them clicked for me. Everyone at the program was excited. He left the residency one night to go to the Golden Globes.

Anyway, I tried to avoid you, but on the third day, I walked into the computer lab and there you were. I was so focused on my apology that I don't remember exactly what you said, but what you said was something like, *I get it. I get it. I'm a teacher, and you're a student*—and I don't remember any of the rest of what you said, but it didn't make sense and it was completely wrong, and I tried to muscle my way through an apology, but you didn't want to hear it. You weren't ready to change your thinking. So, I just left. Maybe I checked my email first.

What I didn't get a chance to tell you is that about three days after that stupid email I sent you, I had this reading at the Latin School, and another book—not the one you were not going to write a blurb for, but a different one you were not going to write a blurb for—was coming out that next spring, and the librarians at school had a nice little reading for me. The librarians were there and faculty, and even a couple of alums—all people who wouldn't have liked me when I was a kid. And there were white tablecloths and wine, and it was so perfect, and that hot washrag around my heart finally went away for a little while.

But on my way home that night, I started thinking about those two me's: the one that had that beautiful reading in the library and the one that sent that email to you. All those people who'd just left my reading sort of thought I was pretty all right, but somewhere you were only thinking about what I dick I was. I get it, though. You get to a point where you think people will finally stop saying shit about your stammer, and I come along like a dickhead and say what I said.

And that's the story I didn't get chance to tell you—or I did tell you, but you didn't want to hear it. Whatever.

Anyway, I can't remember the route I took home from the library reading that night, but somewhere along the way I had to pull over because I couldn't see. Usually it's because of something beautiful or sad that gets me like that, but this was something else. I pulled over because I *couldn't* see, but I was also just *beginning* to see. It was one of those days. It was a reckoning.

Also, perspective sometimes makes me cry like that. Like the day in the Nissan. We were just sitting there eating our beefs and thinking about Kenny George, a sweet giant who is just too big for this world. I'm not kidding about Kenny. He stood flat footed on the court and he curled his fingers around the basketball rim without leaving the ground. He was so big. He was somebody's son, too.

This is probably going to sound crazy, but that night, me and Kane in that Nissan, eating beefs and crying about Kenny George, we were both of us—we were so alive.

The River Above

Margaret Erhart

We give thanks to the Stars who are spread across the sky like jewelry. We see them at night, helping the Moon to light the darkness and bringing dew to the gardens and growing things. When we travel at night, they guide us home. With our minds gathered as one, we send greetings and thanks to all the Stars.
— *From the Haudenosaunee Thanksgiving Address*

I was on the mountain last night, descending in the dark. The dark line of the woods on both sides created a sense of being vulnerable, watched. The air was soft, a March night air without the bite of winter. The wind was up and the clouds scudded quickly toward the north, over the north ridge of the peaks where the kachinas live. Every now and then a bright light shone from the ridge and the snow around me seemed to turn to white ash—an old reminder of an explosive history, a volcano's history.

The night sky revealed itself in pieces, the clouds opening to show the stars and closing again like a hand hiding silver coins. Orion the huntsman lives to the south. He walks across the sky from east to west, following the tracks of rabbits. A quiver of arrows hangs from his belt and in his hands the starry bow. He has a swimmer's shoulders. His feet are planted in the mountain. The clouds shift and lower so I can no longer see him, but I can feel his hunting instinct alive in the dark air. I suddenly feel like all prey must: that to live on the earth is a certainty measurable only breath by breath. The tracks I leave behind in the snow are swept clean in the heave of a second.

Other nights I've stood by water, or slept on it in a boat tied up to shore. Canyons shape the lens. For hours in the dark the movie rolls overhead, a long thin ribbon of film shown frame by frame. One April night on the San Juan after Ellen Meloy's death, the northern lights set sail on a midnight sky—unheard of at that latitude and time of year. Dark pink with bolts of orange leaping upward like visible music. Ellen, hello, I said. It was the river she loved the most and nothing else—the time and place of her appearance—mattered.

Here's a picture: My father at the stern of a hired boat throwing bread to the gulls. Caribbean waters Windex blue, brown-headed Laughing Gulls with a habit of shrieking. Dad tossing whole English muffins their way while the sun settles low, followed quickly by a starry dark. The constellations laid out above like scattered breadcrumbs, random and nameless. There is nothing familiar to me in the sky of the southern hemisphere. I have no anchorage, no mooring, no harbor there where the night sky is not mine. How often I have snapped awake on a beach or in a rocking boat on a river in my own part of the planet and told time by the position of the stars and felt at rights. Or watched a film of cloud smother the moon and felt the shift in weather. Or sensed the river below and the river above as one. They say we can foretell the time and place of our death if we know how to read the sky's prophecies. I don't care to learn this art. I don't care to know.

My father died in January, a bitter night, the night after a flock of birds disabled US Airways flight 1549 and forced a landing in the Hudson River. My mother died in the evening, around supper time, in December. She parted the curtains of early dark and slipped out. She could be unsure in the daylit world, uneasy in finding her earthly way. It was said by some she couldn't find her way out of a hatbox. But give her the stars and she was flawless. Celestial navigation was as natural to her as the next breath. Find Polaris, she'd say. That was our first waypoint. Now Betelgeuse, Altair, Deneb, Vega, then she'd rattle off the planets that shone early and late in our northern sky.

She was a sailor and brought us up to know the things of the sea. Tides, wind, the trim of a sail. And she taught us to find the horizon, to memorize the constellations, to smell land before we saw it and to welcome errant land birds to the rigging where they'd shiver with exhaustion. After she died, among her things I found an old wooden box, teak with a simple latch. Inside, it was padded with blue velvet, cushioning an instrument I had seen in her hands many times before: her sextant. It looked like a cross between a telescope and a protractor. She was good with numbers, good at math, and before GPS became a household word she'd be up on deck at night, sighting Polaris and its distance to the horizon, then by magic she'd know where we were in the world when all around us the world looked to my eyes like a rolling dark sea.

One night camped out on the Esplanade I looked up into the liquid darkness and felt the heaviness of drowning. The luminescent plankton of stars winked on and off above me, and I imagined propelling myself upward, swimming to the surface of the sea in which my body now floated, airless, breathless, and most of all timeless. The heaviness of drowning gave way to the lightness of dying. There was no surface, after all, no separation of this state and that, of breath and no breath. Time was replaced by knowledge. The stars were commas and semicolons in a layered universe that eluded the prison of language. It was a wild night. It felt like my first night on earth, my first night living within the curvaceous bounds of a question mark. The sky offers us this.

One point seven five billion years below the rim, and we know well enough to start early. As we pass by in the dark the sacra datura at the mouth of the first side canyon are blooming. I stop and speak to them, inform them of their beauty, as if they were just created, newly painted and placed there by Georgia O'Keeffe moments ago. Along the way we watch for desert four o'clocks and evening primrose—also creatures of the night. June. The heat by day is well over 100, but time is generous now in the cool dark. The sky tips open as we climb. Sometimes it's no wider than the width of the trail; other times it unfolds above the rattling leaves of the cottonwoods to show us Vulpecula, the little fox to the north, Lupus, the wolf to the south, Canis Major and Minor, Orion's hunting dogs. And on this earth, a band of hungry coyotes yip their frenzied predator language up high in the Horn Creek drainage.

Years ago I joined a band of gringos, scientists interested in the interspecies colonies that grew up in pockets in the volcanic desert environment of the Pinacates, just north of Puerto Peñasco. Elephant tree, senita cactus, brittlebush, cholla, creosote bush. A plant started out solo then gained friends as it drew the sparse rainfall to it, creating moisture and shade and eventually an intimate nursery at its feet. The elephant tree was named for its gray pachydermic bark. When wounded it oozed a thick reddish sap like its cousin frankincense. It was smooth and patriarchal and while it seldom grew larger than bush size, its thick limbs—each one a trunk of its own—stretched out to create a welcoming shade. An invitation. The head scientist, a man called Guy, studied that invitation and the guests that arrived because of it. We were there with tape measures and soil testers, stubby pencils and waterproof notebooks to help gather data and drink some excellent tequila and fall in love with that corner of the desert. Why the notebooks were waterproof I have no idea.

Our first night out in that splendid corner of the Sonora was not quiet. The desert birds and mammals came alive in the cool of night. I came alive too and walked away from camp to be in that greater energy. What I saw surprised me; I had missed it by daylight. The lava that covers most of the Pinacates shone bright black in the moonlight but here and there the marks of passage were clearly visible. These were old pathways across the lava, old human pathways. In the morning I asked Guy about it and he said the trails, invisible by day, needed only be visible at night for that was when the people traveled. Of course. The cool of night. By moon and starlight. The scuff marks of many feet led people where they wanted to go. Night walkers adapted to the desert. Generations of night walkers walking by the light of the Swan, the Sea-goat, the Great Bear.

By the time summer comes, Orion will have chased his rabbits below the horizon and cantankerous Scorpio will scuttle upward into the southern sky. A night on the ridge of the mountain will give the long view in the long light, profiles of cinder hills and the reclining poses of Kendrick, Sitgreaves, Bill Williams—masculine names under which the old names, the native names, the sacred names lie waiting: Dook'o'oosłííd, Gleaming Summit, Abalone Shell Mountain; Nuvátukya'ovi, Place-of-snow-on-the-very-top; Wii Hagnbaja', Moon Mountain, Snowy Mountain; Sunha:kwin K'yabachu Yalanne, Highest Mountain to the West. A rush of wind and the sky darkens as if movement is the instigator of true night. Clouds tearing and mending. Behind them the shreds of constellations we know in whole pieces because where we live we have darkness enough to bring forth light.

The Most Beautiful Woman to Ever Leave Athens, Georgia

Jesse Sensibar

I separated burned bodies from charred helicopter seats and put pieces of seat in blue plastic body bags. I once sent every yellow-flashing construction sawhorse on West Division street flying in a shower of Bondo and rust from the bent body of my fifty-dollar Cadillac. I swapped dope for Harold's fried chicken through barred basement doors. I fell in love with a waitress and people said we lived in a Levi's 501 Blue ad. I was surrounded by girls in black vintage at the Double R Bar beneath the downtown Greyhound station where the Sundowners played until dawn. I smiled as the guy running the chop-shop on my block dumped three Camaro carcasses a week in the vacant lot next door. I drove fast on sweaty nights with a tallboy of Old Style between my thighs and the most beautiful woman to ever leave Athens, Georgia, by my side.

Night Ops

Miranda Dennis

Right before my boyfriend broke up with me, he had been updating me with careful regularity on his and his father's plans to kill the neighbor's dog. I knew very few details about the dog, other than the fact that it was small and yipped. The yipping had bothered my boyfriend's father, a retired physicist with too much genius on his hands and skin that crackled like a small fire if he ate too much gluten. I had never met the man, only seen a photo of him in fluttering khaki shorts on a boat, smoking a cigar amidst the salt spray of New Jersey waters. The face was my boyfriend's face but aged and with a wider jaw, more grizzled and cocksure, a mold he might later pour himself into. *Don't share this photo online,* my boyfriend warned me, as if that could be anyone's first instinct.

Such a man would not easily accept a small dog's tyranny. Maybe I'm too passive myself. Living in Queens I'm confronted by car alarms crying wolf or a passing siren or the rumble of planes landing at two nearby airports. I have learned to be lulled by the sound of car tires in rain, or drunks singing at two a.m., or the occasional bird on my sill singing to its heart's content, as my cat nuzzles as closely as possible to the crack where my sputtering a/c meets the window. A small dog's bark would barely register.

When I met him, my boyfriend was sharing a massive apartment in Crown Heights, Brooklyn, with a mysterious roommate who had a heightened fear of mess, which made him anxious, which made him tiptoe, which made his tall frame seem so small. His block was lined with gray and white London plane trees, those hybrids scaly with the smooth white bark of its sycamore parent, skeletal in winter. But his view from his room overlooked the rooftops of Crown Heights, a church bell outlined by only moonlight, gothic and romantic. He handed me binoculars the first night I saw his apartment, and I looked out from his room, feeling very Hitchcock's *Rear Window* except I couldn't get the focus to work, pressed against my own glasses. My hands shook too much to glimpse beyond the blurred outlines of a city stacked like Legos, so I gave up, pressed the binoculars back to his hands, and positioned myself at the window again to see whatever it was I wasn't seeing.

There was nothing there, just the quiet sleeplessness of the city at night.

When his roommate killed the lease early, a door opened that I didn't want to open: one where a man could grow soft downy feathers on his skinny arms and take flight. As if on cue, he spent time vacillating between living in NYC and moving to the far country, and took short-term rentals to explore what he wanted. One week he stayed at Averne by the Sea, a sprawling apartment complex in Rockaway Beach that had sprung up, inorganic and boxy and clean white lines, after Hurricane Sandy. The inside looked like apartments I had grown up with in Montgomery, Alabama: open layouts, gray carpet, thin walls, just enough light to give you the sense of possibility when you walked into a room, so you'd overlook the weak wood of the cabinets absorbing humidity, or your neighbor coughing through the thin walls. After Sandy had knocked out so much of New York City, had left salt in subway tunnels and eroded the beaches and destroyed lives, this complex was a testament to newness, cleanliness, homogeneity. Many New Yorkers hated it, the way they hate the empty luxury apartments of Long Island City, and while I'm firmly in that camp, the nostalgia of my suburban upbringing hit me hard, especially while at home I dealt with the cracked tiles of my sloping kitchen floor.

The beach was cold and drizzling, everything so gray and dramatic I may as well have been in a foreign country, filmed against a sad soundtrack. Yet I ran up and down the beach, wild as a child, collecting black seashells so perfectly formed I knew I would not be able to hold on to them. Later I scattered them at a coffee shop, in a botanic garden, in the hands of a small child. At the beach I laughed, filming my boyfriend as he sang a sea shanty in his off-key but somehow soothing voice. There was almost no one there, just us, the loud ocean, and the planes heading for JFK. In that moment I said nothing, just laughed. And on he sang: "O no! I'm not a pirate but a man-o-war, cried he/ A sailing down all on the coasts of High Barbary."

"What do you think? Two-bedroom apartments for 2000?" he said, driving us back to the Brooklyn we knew and loved, the crowded streets and strollers parked in cafes. "You think you could ever live in the Rockaways?"

"For a year, I could," I said.

In the space you could hear both of us imagining the other at the beach, one of us just out of frame.

In the Poconos, the Delaware water gap is calm and cold and clear in some places, nestled in soft mountains that promise out-of-towners skiing and lodges that haven't been updated since my birth year, with welcoming green carpets and too much brown. Everything is quiet, once you've bypassed the tourists and built yourself a nice home in the woods. There's only nature, the mystery of which blooms at night, becomes ripe with darkness upon darkness, a tapestry of danger that one can observe from the comforts of one's well-lit living room with a fire roaring. That's the dream. A glass pane separating you from the black bear outside that has come to dig into your trash only to find the can is bear-safe and thus disappointing. Nature is loud, but in alignment with our breath, our heartbeat, our creaking bones. So when some small breed of dog rears its nameless head and barks with abandon, emulating the car alarms of big city living, something must be done about it.

Imagine a physicist for a moment, the kind of man who played with light all day long. Now imagine him, retired and bored, at war with the things he cannot control. Imagine him smoking a cigar on his porch as night falls, the smoke dissipating into the spaces where dusk blurs the horizon. Imagine his peace ripped like nylons by a staccato *yip yip yip*.

And that's when he thought of the bear, under-utilized, yet-to-be-weaponized, a hulking beast who sometimes came sniffing for fast food. My boyfriend's father thought it might be a good idea to start feeding the local bear. Say you take your scraps leftover from dinner—and in their home, there was always a meat for dinner—and you put them out on your property far enough away from your own yard and rather close to your neighbor's. Every day you enjoy a meal with your wife and your adult son who is crashing at your house while he *figures things out*, and after you tidy up you collect the bones and gristle of your meal and take them into the night. If your son must hang around, you enlist him to wear night goggles because it's that kind of family, a family that owns night goggles in the Poconos, as well as fishing poles and hunting rifles and a Swiss army knife. You creep in dead of night to the far edge of your property where it abuts your neighbor's so that you may proffer the bones, like something from a horror movie to summon an erotic Satan, all cloven hooves and abs.

Later, you check each other for ticks, like primates grooming one another.

Next day, you and your son venture out to see, in fact, the scraps are gone. This is good. This is going as planned. The next night you'll head out a little further, a little closer to your neighbor's property, and leave another offering. Then, one day you will stop. You stop feeding the bear, and the bear, hungry and vengeful, will be forced to dine on the nearby dog, his last yip engulfed.

At least, that was the plan. When my boyfriend informed me of this, I laughed it off, mostly because it sounded like something that wouldn't work. If a bear hadn't eaten the dog before, why would it begin now? And didn't bears scare off at the slightest clatter? Still, I received texts about the subject: *just got back from our night ops.* Night ops, as if what they were doing was special and concentrated, required a skillset a marine sniper might have, or an international spy. There they were, pulling their socks high over their ankles to protect themselves from ticks, and walking in the dark like covert operatives.

Update: the men have returned safely from night ops. No bears had eaten them, no ticks buried in them like shrapnel. My boyfriend's bravery had seemed out of character, given his brief time in Brooklyn had proven to rattle his nerves. After his lease was up he bounced from temporary sublets to housesitting gigs in the city to his parents' home in the Poconos. I thought he would return from the mountains, bored and refreshed, ready to eat dim sum and go to shows. I kept it as interesting as I could, in the way that read like every other couple I knew: *let's go to a Mets game/ let's go to Storm King/ let's go see a band play at Brooklyn Steel/ let's walk along the river/ let's eat this specific cuisine you are not likely to find back home/ let me bake for you and cook for you and bring you mason jars full of water/ let me turn you to the light.* Still, his disappearance back home was longer than usual, his texts quick recaps of working on the family's deck re-staining it, on climbing ladders to address gutters, on sneaking bones to bears. It read like a farmer's diary from 1885.

What I wanted was a phone call saying, *I've found this great little spot just an hour outside the city, right on a train line, and I'll be there soon.* To expect him to return to the city would be a bit much, but a compromise might work—a life of commuter lines, glancing up to the constellations peppering Grand Central's ceiling, as a throng of bodies competed for space briefly, briefly, before returning themselves to the greenery running parallel to the Palisades. My dreams of grabbing the

Metro-North, a canvas tote stuffed with an overnight of clothes, were crushed when I received a text saying, *you're a lot of fun, but I'm just not drawn to the city right now.*

I remained a lot of fun, by sheer strength of will. I went to yoga two days in a row. I took nature walks in three of the city's finest parks. I wore a long skirt and gathered it as I climbed the dramatic stone steps up to the Cloisters in Fort Tryon Park, glancing back coyly at the Hudson river which was muddied by spring storms. I lifted my face to the sun, and suffered a burn on my shoulder where it lay uncovered and bare. I drank herbal iced teas and painted my toenails red and emptied out my heart like a change purse. My friends said, *you're too good for him, the way friends do.* I said, *Did I tell you he's trying to kill his neighbor's dog?*

After all this, the dog on the porch is still shouting. It quivers with the fury of needs unmet: a hunger pang, a thirst, the darting of squirrels shaking the branches, indecipherable noise in the shadows while the family sleeps. Maybe, too, it is lonely, left out too long when it wants only to curl up, a diluted wolf burrowed in the family nest. Maybe it senses danger, sees a lanky man on the roof pulling leaves from the gutter, which shower down to another man below. An overwhelming parade of scents: the heavy chemical stain drying in the sun, dew-bent grass steaming by noon, a heady tobacco as the men smoke cigars to celebrate—what? What is it that brings them joy? Will they be sharing it? Will they be marching over here and sharing it? Is it a treat?

And let's not forget, as the men so clearly did, on the life of the bear, who was not designed by nature to be such a pawn. Surely, these men bred by mountains and water, by the soft earth that exhales sweet scent in the summer heat, would know what the bear means in her long lunge towards life.

She treads where she is not supposed to tread, and digs where she is not supposed to dig, and eats whatever she pleases. She should be able to recognize a trap by now, know that it does not always have steel teeth, know that silence belies danger, and that though the men are soft-bodied they are quiet and clever and watching. She should see the bones for what they are, placed unnaturally on a trail made by human hands, but she is very, very hungry.

And she will have her fill.

Wiener Tape

Steve Hughes

The last straw is when my roommate tells everyone that I stole sixty bucks from her dresser. Fuck that! I maybe ate her cookies and her stupid ass Twix bars, but I didn't steal nothing from her dresser. Borrowing is not stealing. I shouldn't have to explain. It is not fair to throw me out. It's extra rotten calling me klepto and spreading lies all over town. Oh man, I am in a real jam. That's when I run into Keisha at the gay bar all done up in a sequined gown, looking totally great. She wears no stuffers or nothing, and she knows how to tape her wiener between her legs for maximum, ladylike effect. Shout out to my girl, Keisha! She is so extra kind to me. When I tell her about my terrible roommate, she says I can crash on her couch. Thank you Keisha! You are so great! I get my stuff. I end up living there for longer than I plan, a lot longer. The whole time, I work hard not to take nothing. Borrow nothing. Not the cash in her nightstand, not her pills, not her weed or cigarettes. I just remind myself over and over: Don't touch! It's hardest when I'm alone in the house. I got a discrepancy with myself. I guess we all do. For sure Keisha does, too. Then it's Friday, and neither of us have dates, so we decide to hit the town together. I sit on her bed, popping these little frozen éclairs, watching her get dressed. I ask about her wiener—I mean, does it hurt having it all folded backwards between her legs? Nope, she says, long as it don't get hard. What then? I say. She raises her eyebrows just about as high as they go and smiles at me. I bet you've got a nice wiener, I say. Eh, she says, It's just a nothing special, run-of-the-mill wiener. Then she says I can wear her earrings, and here's some big bangles to ride on my wrists, and try these sexy heart-shaped sunglasses, too. She shimmies into her cocktail dress and pulls on a wig of long black hair that drops over her shoulder blades. Then she looks at me, rubs her chin, and digs a dress from her closet. Try this on, she says. I change in front of her mirror. Only thing is, it's a little snug on my butt. Damn girl, she says, You are so lucky to have a butt. It's a nothing-special butt, I say. Funny, but everything I'm wearing tonight is hers, even the shoes. I didn't have to ask. She just gave it all to me. From sheer kindness, Keisha is helping me become a brand new girl. She's so sweet. Finally, we hit the bar. We sit on stools, feeling beautiful, hoping for just the right man to find us. Look at us together—are we not soul sisters? Slurping up Long Islands, glowing in the black light. This stuff we're drinking is like magic. After a couple, we forget about men, and head back to her house. I help her out of her dress and peel off the tape that hides her. She snaps forward like on a spring and thraps against her belly. After my dress is finally off, she plunks a finger in my tighty-mighty and moves real slow, just floating on me with the nicest rocking motion. That night Keisha becomes my king, my queen. In the morning, we wake in her bed, our mascara smeared on the pillows. We lie there both feeling so happy. I'm thinking maybe this is it. Like, she might be the one. She might be my man.

Jesus and His Bad Headache

Steve Hughes

The school gives us boys clip-on ties to wear. They dig a red mark into my neck. I hate Catholic school and big fat Miss Marion, too. She makes us pray, then say the pledge of allegiance. Everything about her is so mean. Today is special, she says, Because the new holy cards are here. She passes them out. Mine has a picture of Jesus with hair to his shoulders and a scrappy beard. Lines of light stick like blades from his skull as if he's got a bad headache. A bunch of kids have gathered around him. Maybe that's why his head hurts. Jesus has his hand in the air, like it's moving away from his mouth to pull more words out, or hold something, maybe an old piece of fruit, maybe Eve's dirty apple, maybe both her apples, soft and evil, so he can go to hell too. Even so young, I know of things like Eve. I have a pen with a lady on it. You hold it one way and her clothes peel off. Flip it back and she is dressed. Sometimes there is nothing to do but think of Miss Marion and wonder how she would look if all the buttons of her white shirt popped and the zipper of her skirt burst apart, and everything suddenly opened and dropped. Probably, naked, she'd be a lot less mean. I flip my holy card over. On the back it says the Ten Commandments For Children. Love your schoolmates is number one. I look at Jeffery. Just yesterday, he socked me in the shoulder for no reason. I'll never love him, no matter what. Then Miss Marion announces it's time for a bathroom break. Because I sit in the back, I am last to go, and for a couple seconds, I have the room to myself. I look at the new holy cards, sitting on the empty desks. I move fast. I grab them all, ripping them as I shove them in my pocket. Then I wait in the hall with rest of the class. Miss Marion is there, hands on her hips, big wrinkly boobers hiding under her monster bra. Double chin. Her giant crushing butt makes an umbrella out of her skirt. If it rained and you went under there for shelter, you would surely die from the poison gas that bleeds from her butt. When it's my turn in the boy's room, I empty my pockets. I drop the precious cards right in the urinal. They float in everyone else's unflushed pee. Then I pull out my dinger and spray them good. This is the beginning of all sorts of trouble. It doesn't take long for Miss Marion to come slamming down on me. She grabs my shoulder, yanks me into the hall, and yells my full name for everyone to hear. You are a heretic! She hollers, It's a blasphemy! You hear me, a blasphemy! Get out of my sight! Get out! Now, I am going to Hell. That's for sure. But first, I need to go sit in the principal's office. He doesn't understand what might be wrong with me. He calls my mother at work and makes her come get me. I slump in the chair as he tells her about the consequences of suspension but then decides it's better to simply kick me out of school forever. He even asks for my tie back. I pull it from my collar and drop it on his desk, then stand there between them, holding my fingers to the welt on my neck.

The Sexy Stillness of Church

Steve Hughes

I meet my date—ready for this—at the Port Bar, the weird one on Joseph Campau with a sign out front that looks like it might have been made for a vineyard. Food/Spirits, it says, but there is no food here, just whiskey and beer and cheap wine. So, those three large fish on the sign, swimming, mouth to tail, one about to gulp down the other, might be what really happens here. The food eats itself. Maybe the patrons do too. I find my date in a booth opposite the bar. I apologize for my scruffy appearance. It's just been such a busy day at the restaurant, but he doesn't seem to mind. He is short and in good shape for a guy in his late 40s. He says he moved here from the U.P., Iron River. Then he lets slide that he is a priest. What? I say, No way! For real, he says. He shows me his ID. In the photo, he's wearing a collar with a little white square at the base of his throat. Wow! Holy shit, I say, Do you keep that in your car? Your priest outfit? No, he says, Not the robe. Just the collar. You know, in case I have to go on a hospital visit. I ask if he could wear it tonight. I mean, it's just a total turn on. He smiles, but says No, maybe another time. After a couple drinks, all I want to do is confess to him. I'm wracking my brain for some mortal sin. Have I not been thinking about this for years? I mean as a boy I was so attracted to my priest. I dreamed about the darkness of the confessional booth. As if a little door in there could slide open, and screen be removed to allow priest and parishioner to join hands. Or maybe other more significant parts might pitch from one dark space to the next to be held and kissed, there in the sexy stillness of church. Because it's getting late, I pay our tab and we exit the Port. Standing in front of the sign with its lush suggestion of what the bar could be but is definitely not, my date invites me to his place. It's up in Southfield actually. It's one those priest houses that connects to a church—whatever they are called. I try again to get him to put on his robes, but he won't do it. I tell you, though. We have really good sex. It's super hot. This all happens up by the old Northland mall which is where my Mom took me as a kid. One time in the toy store, she said I could get anything I wanted. We were in the aisle with the rugged little GI Joe figures with all their army equipment like guns and jeeps and helicopters. I didn't want any of it. I took her to the next aisle and I picked out a do-it-yourself stencil kit for decorating clothes. The pink sides of the box were patterned with flowers. You're sure, Mom said. I mean, I was and I wasn't. I'm certain it was a dead giveaway.

All Dressed Up and Nowhere

Steve Hughes

We are late for her friend's annual Halloween party, me and Frida. She is tapping her foot about the slow elevator. It's a dorm, I say, What do you expect? She doesn't answer, but just looks at her phone. My full-body robot costume is annoying her, too. It makes navigating the lobby complicated. Even getting out the door is an issue. I mean, my head is a bucket with a hole cut in it. I can't see real good or walk much either. I can only duck walk, but I do look awesome, just super cumbersome. I am really needing her guidance. I mean, Could you please just hold on to my hand! But she says it doesn't go with her costume. Holding hands doesn't. Frida is dressed as a Star Trek alien like from the 70s. A metallic fabric crosses her shoulders, reaches down from her neck and cups her breasts, leaving her belly exposed, so everyone can see her stylish navel-ring. She is dazzling, sparkling, amazing. She out-classes me by miles. This is true even out of costume. Everyone knows it. Frida knows it. My dad, running his Deli, slicing meat behind bulletproof glass, knows it too. Her dad flying around the country to give expensive advice to company people—whatever. Thing is, Frida keeps letting go of me. My clunky cardboard robot fingers reach for hers, batting her by accident. Quit, she says, I'm texting. I'm telling them we're late. The party started like hours ago. I remind her that I can't barely see. I need help and all. She doesn't say she can't hear me. We are on Woodward, walking right into the noise of traffic. I thought we were together but her hand is nowhere. I'm out there, suddenly confused about the lines of the crosswalk. Calling her name. She's not answering. I can hear plenty of voices, but not hers. Then cars start honking. I realize they are honking at me. Get out of the road idiot! You idiot! You dumb fuck robot! I am stuck. Frida is gone. She has no idea. I am calling for her. Shouting into my bucket head.

The Opposite of Love

Alexis Bowe

It's drizzling as I descend the concrete steps of the Western Springs Metra station. I consider turning around and hopping on the next train back to Chicago, but then I see my mom's big black Escalade pulled up to the curb waiting for me and I know that I can't turn back because there's a chance she saw me too.

As I approach her car, I get a view of her license plate and am reminded of how fucking stupid it is: ESCALADY. She thought it was so funny and clever when she got it changed. That was back when she had a sense of humor, however lame it may have been. Back before my dad died. She's always been cold, but after my dad passed away, whatever warmth she did have iced over completely.

I sigh and get in one last good eye roll before climbing into the car.

She's applying a second coat of that hideous coral lipstick she loves so much when I get in, and she doesn't look away from her task to say hi to me. "Hello, Olivia," she greets me, eyes still locked on her reflection. She closes up her tube of lipstick and puckers her lips in the sun-visor mirror, making sure they're perfect before she flips it back up.

"Hi, Mom," I reply.

She turns to me, and I can see where the blush she's wearing has begun to cake into the fine lines on the apples of her cheeks. "I'm so glad you could make it." She pauses, glances in the back seat, realizes I'm by myself. I feel my pulse quicken. "Where's Brad?" she asks, and I can already hear the disappointed inflection in her voice.

"He's sick," I tell her. She stares at me for a moment. I maintain an even expression, though the back of my neck has begun to prickle with sweat.

"Well, that's too bad," she finally says, and I can tell she hasn't decided whether or not she actually believes me yet. "I was really looking forward to seeing him again."

"I know," I say. "He told me to tell you he's sorry he couldn't make it, but he wanted you to have this since he wasn't able to come."

I reach into the backpack I brought with me and pull out the expensive bottle of white wine that Brad had left at my apartment prior to dumping me. I hate white wine, and I knew that my mom wouldn't believe my "he's sick" bullshit that easily, so I figured this was the perfect opportunity to put this disgusting pinot grigio to use.

Her face lights up. "Oh, he remembered! At our holiday party last year, he and I were talking about how much I love a good pinot grigio," she tells me, as if I wasn't standing right next to them when this conversation took place.

She smiles sentimentally at the bottle and for a minute, I think she might start crying. Maybe this wasn't such a good idea after all. Now, when I eventually do tell her that Brad isn't sick, just sick of me, she's going to be even more upset.

"This bottle isn't cheap either," she continues. "That boyfriend of yours sure does have good taste."

"Yep," I reply. I stuff the bottle back inside my backpack, and my mom checks her reflection one last time in the rearview mirror before driving away.

I sit in my childhood bedroom while my mom straightens up and prepares appetizers downstairs. I didn't offer to help, not because I didn't want to, but because my mom likes everything done how she wants it done, so I would've just ended up getting in her way. And also I kind of didn't want to.

I grab the flask of Jameson I brought with me out of my backpack and take a swig. Today is my dad's birthday. Every year since my dad died, my mom has hosted these really strange birthday parties for him where she invites all of my parents' friends and our extended family over, and we all have dinner and tell our favorite stories about my dad, and to cap the night off, my mom brings out a huge birthday cake, candles and all, and we light it and sing happy birthday to him, and then my mom blows out the candles. It's really fucking weird. I take another swig from my flask.

Sighing, I lean back on my elbows and glance around my room, a smile tugging at the corners of my mouth. Posters of bands like Taking

Back Sunday, Brand New, Rage Against The Machine, and Nirvana are hung up all over my walls. My wooden desk is graffitied with stickers from Zumiez and Sharpie drawings done by teenage me (a marijuana leaf, a hand holding up a middle finger, the words *fuck the system*). If I were to open the drawers of my dresser, I'd find countless pairs of ripped-up skinny jeans and a whole bunch of wrinkled band T-shirts. I thought I was a real badass back in the day, rimming my eyes with heavy black eyeliner, smoking Newports out my window at night after my parents went to sleep, dying my hair pink then blue then purple with Manic Panic hair dye, then teasing it so it stood an inch high on my head.

My mom hated it. She wanted me to be the cheerleader or the girl in AP classes or the girl on the speech team when I was in high school. Instead, I was the girl who got caught smoking a joint in the bathroom, the girl who ditched school one day to go lose my virginity to this skater kid named Matt on the couch in his parents' garage.

Ding dong.

I hear the doorbell ring downstairs, meaning the first guest has arrived. *Fuck.* I take another long swig, then pop a piece of gum in my mouth to mask the whiskey smell.

"Olivia, would you come down please?" my mom calls from the bottom of the stairs. "Aunt Donna and Uncle Raymond are here!"

Aunt Donna is my dad's sister and she's a real fucking bitch. She works at the DMV and is allergic to just about everything (dogs, cats, dust, peanuts . . . the list goes on). When I was twelve, I asked my parents to buy me a kitten for Christmas, and they were going to except that Aunt Donna convinced them not to. She came up with all these excuses about how I wasn't responsible enough to take care of a cat and how my parents were the ones who would end up having to clean up after it. But I knew that she really didn't want us to get a cat because she was allergic and didn't want her eyes to get all red and itchy every time she came to visit. I never forgave her for that.

I trudge down the stairs, already wishing that I would've told my mom that I was the one who was sick and not come at all. When I reach the bottom of the staircase, Aunt Donna and Uncle Raymond are standing there waiting to greet me.

Aunt Donna's mousy brown hair is tucked behind her head in a tight bun. She always wears her hair like this, as if she's embarrassed to have it or something. She's got this ugly ruched top on that I bet the JCPenney saleslady told her would hide her stomach, but it really just accentuates it.

"Hi," I say to her.

She pulls her chapped lips up into a strained smile and says, "Hello, Olivia."

I turn to Uncle Raymond, a bald, bland man, and say hello to him too. Then we all file into the kitchen and sit around the table, my mom and Aunt Donna sipping that pinot grigio I brought, and my Uncle Raymond and I each sipping one of the Blue Moons that he brought. My mom and Aunt Donna chat away, but both Uncle Raymond and I sit in silence.

One everlasting hour later, all the guests have arrived and my mom has moved everyone into the dining room, where we all sit around the dark stained mahogany dining table.

My mom lets everyone know that dinner will be served shortly, and she rises from her seat next to me to make her annual toast that she begins all of these birthday dinners for my dad with. The room falls silent and all eyes go to her, standing there with her wine glass in hand and a sad, far-off look in her eyes.

"As always, I'd like to start by thanking all of you for coming," she begins. "I can't believe it's been four years already. Roger would be forty-eight today." She smiles a small, sad smile, and her eyes become glassy with tears. "I just know that he's looking down on all of us gathered here together, and he's smiling. I am so grateful to all of you for coming here to celebrate Roger's life with me. When Roger passed, he took a piece of me with him. I truly don't know how I would have gotten through it if not for all of you, which is why today, I'd like to go around and give out a personal thank you to each person who stuck by me during this difficult time."

She begins going around the table, giving out personal thank yous to everyone, beginning with Aunt Donna, then moving to my grandma, then to her snooty country club friends. I start to zone out, not having any interest in listening to my mom's artificial gratitude, but then she looks down at me and says, "And lastly, I'd like to thank my beautiful daughter, Olivia."

My cheeks go warm at the sound of my name. What could she possibly have to thank me for?

"I know that your dad's passing hit me pretty hard, so I wasn't really able to be there for you when it happened. You handled it so well, though, and were so strong. You let me grieve and held it together for me, and I really admire you for that. I always thought that you got your strength from you father."

I stare at the table in front of me, my shoulders squared, chest thumping. She *admires* me? She probably didn't mean that. She's probably just saying it so everyone else will admire her for what a kind and humble mother she is.

"Well, I won't bore you all with my babbling on anymore," she laughs. "Happy birthday, Roger."

"Happy birthday, Roger," everyone at the table echoes, clinking their glasses together with the people beside them. We all take a sip, and then the neighbor boy that my mom hired to be the server for the night comes into the dining room, rolling a tray of food in with him.

We're on the second course of the four course meal my mom has prepared for us and so far, nothing too terrible has happened. My mom and her country club friends have carried on vapid, gossipy conversation, and I've mostly kept quiet, only speaking when responding to a question my mom or one of her friends directed my way. I managed to only roll my eyes twice while listening in on their talk of some lady at the country club named Polly who never lost that baby weight and that new restaurant with that *divine* gluten free flatbread and that poor Judy whose babysitter is sleeping with her husband. In my mind, I imagined stuffing one of the whole wheat dinner rolls into each of their mouths so that they'd all just shut the fuck up for a few minutes.

Now, as we finish up our kale salads and prepare for the salmon that is coming next, Karen spoon-feeds yogurt to her baby, who sits in a high chair that she brought from home next to her seat.

Karen is only thirty-four, more than a decade younger than my mom and exactly one decade older than me, and she had one last baby after getting remarried to her new husband because they wanted a child of their own. She already had three children with her first husband, so this little guy is her fourth. The thought of having four children makes me feel physically ill, but Karen told my mom she wishes she could have had one more.

"Oh Karen, he is just precious," my mom gushes as she watches her dab the baby's face with a napkin. "Olivia, isn't he just precious?" she asks me, and I know that this is her passive aggressive way of reminding me that I don't have a precious child of my own for her to fawn over.

"Yep," I reply flatly. "Super precious."

My mom turns back to Karen. "How old is he now?"

"Twenty-four months," Karen replies, her face beaming with pride over this pudgy, sticky-fingered human that she's created.

"He's fucking two," I utter under my breath before I can stop myself.

Karen's big blue eyes go wide, and she lets out a polite, nervous laugh. "Pardon me?" she says, even though I know she heard me.

"I said your baby is fucking two," I repeat, loud enough now that Aunt Donna all the way at the other end of the table looks up and shoots me a disapproving glare.

I feel my mom tense up beside me, and she begins to apologize profusely. "I am so sorry, Karen," she says. "Please don't mind Olivia. She can be very . . . temperamental."

Karen's mouth still hangs slightly ajar, and all the other guests at the table try to hide the fact that they're all watching this play out. They sneak glances out of the corners of their eyes, then turn back to whoever they came with to whisper about Linda's *temperamental* daughter.

I feel my mom's bony hand land on my shoulder, and I know that I'm about to get a stern talking to about how to behave around company. "Olivia," she mutters to me through her teeth. "A word, please?"

She turns back to her guests, flashing them all a wide Miss America smile, assuring them that there is no need to worry, that everything is just fine. She's always been great at keeping it together in front of company, no matter how pissed off or upset she is. It's one of the many traits I didn't inherit from her.

She rises from her seat and stares down at me until I rise from my own. Then I follow her out of the dining room and into the living room, where she keeps her shrine of my father.

Against the wall adjacent to the one with the entertainment center is a large wooden table topped with candles, a vase full of roses (the flowers that my father brought my mother on their first date), and framed photos of my parents together. A photo of them at their high school prom together, my mom wearing a big pink dress. A photo of them on their wedding day, my mom wearing an even bigger white dress. A photo of them in the hospital right after I was born, my mom wearing her favorite coral lipstick and a light coat of mascara because apparently giving birth isn't even a good enough excuse not to look perfectly presentable. And on the wall behind this table hangs a large photo in a gold frame of my parents and me on Christmas, back when I was only eight and not a massive disappointment. We're all wearing matching shades of red, and I'm smiling a tight, closed-lip smile because I was missing a tooth at the time and my mom said that the gap in my teeth was unsightly, that she didn't want me to expose it in the picture by smiling with my teeth.

My mom walks over to this shrine of hers and stands right there in front of it to begin her scolding. I stand next to her as she stares at her wall of photos, letting out a deep sigh.

"Olivia," she begins, turning to look at me, "I don't know what to do with you anymore. I just don't understand why you feel the need to be so rude all the time. It's your father's birthday, for God's sake. The least you could do is be respectful. Your father and I raised you better than this."

I roll my eyes. I wonder how long it would take me to walk to the train station from here. It's only about two miles away, three at the most. It shouldn't take me more than forty-five minutes. I wonder if it's still raining out.

"Olivia," my mom snaps. "Are you even listening to me?"

"What's there to listen to?" I remark, and I feel stupid because I actually let myself start to believe that maybe my mom really did secretly admire me like she said she did in her little speech. "I've heard this a thousand times. I'm rude. I'm temperamental. I'm not polite enough. I don't dress nice enough. I curse too much. I don't even know why you still invite me here if you hate me so fucking much."

I cross my arms over my chest and stare back at her, with her neatly ironed dress and her tall, hairspray-hard hair. Her green eyes, the same peridot color as my own, are narrowed at me, and her coral lips are pressed into a tight line.

"Olivia, I do not hate you," she says. "I just wish that you weren't so . . . unpleasant all the time. It's as if you enjoy setting me off or something, like you're just looking to get a rise out of me. I hope you don't act this way around Brad."

My stomach dips at the sound of Brad's name.

"God bless that man for putting up with these attitudes of yours. He may find them cute or charming, but I don't."

"Well, apparently neither does he, because he broke up with me," I blurt out.

Her face goes stone cold. She says nothing. I glance to my right, look into my beaming eight-year-old eyes, and wish I could be that young again. Wish I could just start over and maybe not fuck things up as much this time.

"What did you do?" my mom finally says, her voice barely audible.

I turn back to her. "What?" I remark.

"What did you do?" she asks again, raising her voice. "You must have done something. What, did you cheat on him? Pick fights with him like you do with me? What was it?"

"I didn't *do* anything," I hiss at her, and I want to tell her how I actually tried this time. How I apologized after yelling at him instead of just pretending it didn't happen. How I smiled and made small talk when I met his parents on Thanksgiving. How I did everything I thought I was supposed to do to make it work. How even at my best, I still was not good enough. But I know she wouldn't believe me, anyways, so instead I save my breath.

"Well, you must have done something," she replies. She shakes her head, crosses her thin arms over her chest. "Brad was so good for you. He had a job, he was polite and respectful, he was well educated . . . I thought you were really going to turn your life around with him." Her eyes cloud over with disappointment. "I should've known it wouldn't last."

"Well, if you love him so much, then you fucking date him," I snap. "I'm not going to sit here and listen to you talk about what a fuck-up I am, though. I'm leaving."

I shove past her and run up the stairs into my old bedroom to grab my things. When I reach my backpack, I immediately go for my flask of whiskey and down a long sip.

"Jesus Christ," I hear my mom's ice cold voice from behind me. I turn to find her standing in the doorway, arms crossed over her chest, disgust crinkling her brow. "Is this why he broke up with you? Are you abusing substances again?"

And I want to scream, cry, yell, rage, but I don't. Instead, I press my lips together and squeeze my eyes shut. I breathe in deeply through my nose and try to ground myself like Anna taught me in our last therapy session. I hold my breath, count to five, then let it out, slowly, through my mouth.

"What are you doing?" my mom asks me.

But I refuse to tell her I've started going to therapy, so instead, I open my eyes, take another deep breath, and grab my backpack, slinging it onto my back. My hands are shaking at my sides, and I wish that my mom would just go back downstairs so I could leave in peace, but she remains blocking the doorway.

"Please move so that I can leave," I say to her.

She stares back at me, not budging. "Why did you lie to me?" she asks.

"What?" I remark.

"You told me that Brad was sick, that that was why he couldn't come today. Why did you lie to me?"

I feel my eyes roll. I just want to go home. I can't be here anymore. I can't stand here and talk to my mom about Brad. That little breathing exercise only works so well. I can feel myself ready to break, though, and I don't want to do it here.

"I'm not talking to you about this right now," I reply, keeping my tone low and even. "Now please move so that I can leave."

"I'm not moving until you answer my question. Why did you lie to—"

"Because it's easier than telling you the truth!" I snap before she can finish getting her full question out. "Look how you reacted when I told you Brad and I broke up! You immediately blamed me just like you always do. I knew you would react that way, and I didn't want to make today even more unbearable than it already was going to be."

She stares back at me, her lips forming a tight line. "Well, you did say that *he* broke up with *you*, so it's only natural for me to assume that you must have done something to cause him to do that," she finally says. "And that's rather rude of you to call you father's birthday unbearable."

I feel the tightness closing in on my chest, and I know that if I don't leave, I will boil over and erupt. "I'm done talking to you about this. Please. Move."

My teeth are clenched behind closed lips and my nails dig into the palms of my hands. She hesitates for a moment before shaking her head and turning around to go back downstairs. I stand there in my room for a moment after she leaves, allowing tears to well up in my eyes. Only for a moment, though. A moment is all that she gets from me. She deserves no more than that.

I blink them away and descend the stairs. I can already hear my mom, back in the dining room, laughing amongst her guests. I imagine her coming back into the room and smiling that pageantry smile of hers, apologizing to all of them for the disruption, assuring them that the disruption has left now, asking them to please don't let that ruin the rest of their evening.

I roll my eyes and slip out through the front door.

It's still raining, so I pull the hood of my sweatshirt up over my head and pull on the strings until it tightens around my face. I drink my whiskey as I walk, but it doesn't feel like it's doing its job. I keep drinking it anyways until the flask is empty and my skin is buzzing and my rage has dulled to just a phantom of anger.

Harvest Time

B.L. Makiefsky

Jesse peered out the window and saw Mrs. Wilcox, the caseworker who wouldn't give his mother bus tickets home. This was huge. He blamed Mrs. Wilcox for being stuck in Michigan, and not on the bus to Texas. Now he thought of paying her back. He didn't much care how that came about as he propelled himself on his crutches through the corridors of Lakeshore Hospital to his room that evening. He could only guess how good it would make him feel when it did.

He had drifted in and out of consciousness that first night. At first dreams unfolded slowly in endless loops of touchdown glory on his home field in Donna, Texas. He moved effortlessly, scoring at will each time he touched the ball. Then in a flash he lay in a heap outside the lines, the weight of the world on his leg. He felt himself to be in a hurry. To go where? The weight and the waiting were unbearable. And then— nothing. A nurse's mouth opened and closed and her words came from a different place than her lips. Jesse thought he cried out, but his own voice went unheard. The nurse held something in her hand. His wrist. Someone's wrist. He observed this from where he floated above his bed, looking down at the boy in it. Then—men in gloved hands pulling a rope. Voices. Bells. A clanging of pots and pans. He felt alone in this strange place, and as his fear abated, he felt a giddiness, too, as the curtain lifted and the new day cast yet another spell.

"Jesse," his mother, Sarita, said, suddenly in his face, a hand on his forehead. She waited. "Jesse. The drugs put you out. Jesse?"

A nurse introduced herself as Marie. She was short and stout with a nest of curly dark hair. "Do you remember what happened?" she said.

"Do you know where you are?" There was a gap in her upper front teeth and she whistled when she spoke. "The hospital," Marie continued. "Are you in pain?"

Jesse's leg was bandaged, his elbow pinned down by what felt like a nail running through it. "My head hurts," he finally said, with great effort. "My arm, too."

Marie adjusted the IV attached there. She said that the emergency doctor had cleaned his leg, removing splinters left by a crate of apples. Nothing broken. He could have breakfast if he wanted. Or just a popsicle.

"When do we go back to Texas?" said Jesse. He thought of football, his grandfather, the skinny girl Alicia from Reynosa, who had waved good-bye in April.

Marie looked at Sarita. "The doctor explained to your mother. He closed part of the wound. You'll need more tests when the swelling is down. To see if there was nerve damage."

"Nerve damage," sighed Sarita, "is when you find your child on the pavement bleeding."

Marie said that the resident would look at the leg again soon. Then she'd change the dressing. The wound was draining. She asked Sarita if she needed a place to stay. Sarita said that Marty King from Human Services had found a family where she could live temporarily.

Sarita watched Marie and an aide transfer Jesse into a wheelchair. "He's got to start moving," Marie said. "Even if just this." They kept his leg elevated.

The nurse asked Sarita if she remembered what the emergency doctor said. She read from her laptop as the aide finished positioning Jesse. ". . . forklift tore patient's flesh, above right knee. X-rays negative. Crush injury not ruled out . . . possible compression of muscle tissue." Marie indicated the IV and said that the doctor had ordered an antibiotic and anti-inflammatory along with a painkiller. The wound would have to be cleaned frequently. More stitches would be required. He'd get a tetanus shot, too.

"His shots are current," said Sarita, reaching into her purse for Jesse's records. "Just a booster," said Marie. "A precaution." She asked Jesse to hold the IV pole as Sarita wheeled him from the room.

The next day a nurse with red hair cleaned the wound, changed the dressing and said that a specialist would examine him. She said that it was a miracle that his muscles, tendons, and blood vessels were not cut. Maybe he could go home soon. She removed the IV.

"I live in Texas," Jesse said.

She gave Jesse crutches, and the freedom to move on his own as long as the swelling continued to go down. Maneuvering came easy to him; his arms were strong from working in the orchard. Mr. Gray, the grower, had even called him *podersoso ratón*, mighty mouse. Still, Jesse's leg gave him an uneasy feeling. At times his toes went numb. He wandered the corridors of the small two-story hospital when Sarita wasn't there, poking around the old building, finding doors locked and unlocked. He had visited a hospital once before, to see his grandmother. She never came home. Now he propped his crutches against a wall and pushed on a door which opened to a closet-like room where crisp white coats hung wall to wall. He fingered one, a coat much like any doctor might wear.

"Go ahead," said Marie behind him. "Try it on."

"Were you following me?" said Jesse, startled.

"To keep you out of trouble." He leaned on her as she put the crutches aside and helped him into the jacket. It reached his knees, but another nurse passing by said that he looked darling and insisted that he keep it on. She rolled up the sleeves to his wrists and pinned them. Jesse followed Marie to a desk where she made a tag, *Jesse Madrigal, Chief of Operations*, and stuck it to his lapel. "Your third day here," said Marie. "And already you're at the top of the heap." Jesse decided to hide the coat in his room where Sarita would not find it.

Later that afternoon, when he catapulted himself past the nurses' station, Marie called out to him. "Sit, my dear friend, and listen to this." She read from the Bear County newspaper. "'It was the first accident at Northland Cannery in seven years, and—although the numbers are not in yet—the late season apple crop promises to be the best in a decade. The twelve-year-old migrant boy likely didn't hear the forklift above the din of the heavy trucks leaving the lot for market. X-rays were negative, and he has made many friends at Lakeshore Hospital.'" Marie looked up at Jesse. "Front page stuff. You're famous."

Jesse smiled and eyed the pizza box alongside her paperwork. She warmed up a piece for him. "Who told the newspaper all that?" he said.

"The reporter was here. He talked to me, and your mother. There isn't much else to report on in these parts."

"Do you like it that way?"

Marie was silent for a time. "Quiet is good," she said at last. "People come here to forget the places they leave. Vacation homes near Lake Michigan for some. Hiding out for others." She took the remainder of the pizza and walked off. When she didn't return, Jesse lingered for a few minutes.

That was about right, he thought. Rounded a corner—and bam! Didn't see or hear the forklift. He wondered why the reporter didn't ask *him*; talking to adults came easy to Jesse. He often translated documents for older workers in the orchards and fields, and phone calls to distant grandchildren who didn't speak Spanish. Other times he helped out at Peter Gray's office, explaining to workers deductions for this or that on payday. Probably the same reporter who had interviewed his mother after the squash, he thought. He seemed to like Sarita; a lot of men did.

Just then he heard the chirp of a siren. Jesse jammed his crutches hard into the floor, propelling himself to a window across from the entrance to the emergency room. Outside, hospital lights cut into the falling dark and the street was quiet. A few geese skittered along the pond on the hospital grounds as an ambulance came to a stop. A man and a woman in uniforms got out, opened the rear doors, and wheeled a patient out. Under the bright lights he saw her, Betty Wilcox, plain as day, and as helpless as a newborn. *Stupid lady*, thought Jesse. *We just wanted to go home.*

"A neighbor found her," a voice said, startling him. He turned to see an orderly, and wondered if he had followed him, too. "She'd fallen," the clean-cut young man said.

Jesse returned to his room. Seeing Mrs. Wilcox had set his heart pounding. He wondered if she'd stay at the hospital, and if so, where? He couldn't wait to ask her, *how are you feeling?* Of course, he'd be pretending. He didn't care how she felt. She was a whacko. And he'd say, *wouldn't you rather be home?* Maybe then she'd get it. They had only asked for bus tickets to Texas. Sarita's arrival interrupted his thoughts. She had heard from the doctor that his leg was draining well, and the swelling had subsided. Her ride to the hospital waited outside now to take her shopping. She'd be back.

Jesse lay in bed with his leg elevated, trying to read *The Adventures of Tom Sawyer,* which his teacher had sent over. The words, however, seemed to jump all over the page. Then the wall behind him hummed. He grabbed his crutches and looked into the hallway, just as the elevator doors opened. The same orderly wheeled a patient on a gurney past his door. A couple and a younger man followed. Several rooms near Jesse's were occupied but never had visitors, and another room toward the end of the hall had been empty from day one.

It was there where Betty Wilcox was left.

Jesse waited, perched in his doorway. A short time later, he heard the visitors leave Mrs. Wilcox's room. "She doesn't get it," the younger man said. "She'll be okay," said the older one. "I'm worried," said the woman, as the three disappeared in the elevator. The hospital floor was laid out like a small "t," with the nurses' station at the cross and usually deserted after eight o'clock. Seeing no one, Jesse now slipped on his white coat and quietly propelled himself down the hall. He peered into the caseworker's room, surprised that it was smaller than his own. Mrs. Willcox lay in bed, a patch over one eye, a bruise on her forehead. He hopped closer. Her perfectly combed hair wasn't so perfect anymore. She appeared to be asleep, her torso attached to a web of cords and tubes. *Like a helpless bug,* thought Jesse. He leaned over her bed for a moment and thought, too, that he might free her, using his crutch like a magic wand to make all that protruded from Betty Wilcox disappear.

He watched the blinking of the monitors that she was connected to, the only bright things under the dim light. Then she opened her one eye wide.

"Are you the resident?" Mrs. Wilcox said. "Please. Are you?" She stared out from her bed covers like a frightened child. "I don't want to go to Grand Rapids to see the neurologist," she said, grabbing the hem of Jesse's coat. "Please," she said, again. Jesse marveled at this small, plump fist that held fast to his borrowed coat. He thought it marvelous, too, that this woman who he blamed for his family's troubles was now so in need herself.

"What is it?" he said anxiously. "What do you want?"

"Please, doctor. I can't do this anymore."

For the first time Jesse understood the real significance of the coat he wore. He thought of tossing it in the corner, and running. If he could. But he only removed the woman's hand, leaned back on his crutches, puffed his chest out, and said: "Is this an emergency, Mrs. Wilcox?"

"Yes, I suppose it is."

"An *eh-mer-hencia*," Jesse said slowly, pronouncing the word in Spanish and then parroting the words Mrs. Wilcox had used at her office, "is something unforeseen, something that you can't predict."

Mrs. Wilcox said that she wasn't feeling well. She didn't understand.

"*No hay emergencia!*" Jesse said. "You had your whole life to get better. And not be the person you are." He wasn't sure why the words came out that way. Hearing them reminded him of the feeling he had when he was looking down at himself that first night at the hospital; it was, and wasn't him. He didn't know what to believe, then or now, and was overcome by sorrow. For his messed-up leg, and all the touchdowns he wouldn't score in Pop Warner. For not being able to wrestle his grandfather. For not being on the bus home. For wanting to tear from Betty Wilcox what he thought she'd taken from him.

Mrs. Wilcox wet her lips with her tongue. She squinted out of her one eye, and raised her arm as if to block the little light there was. "Are you my doctor?"

"I am Jesse Madrigal. You didn't approve our application. Denied us bus tickets home."

"I don't want to live," said Betty, looking away. "Help me."

Bingo! thought Jesse. He gleefully imagined the reporter's next headline: *It was the first accident at the hospital in seven years . . .*

"What do you need?" asked Jesse.

"Bring me that bag." Jesse didn't move. "Over there. On the chair," she said, in a tone—even in her weakened state—reminding him of her office and everything he didn't like about her. "My purse," Mrs. Wilcox said.

Jesse turned to the chair by the window. On the sill above it he saw a vase of roses, and a card, which was open. *Betty, Come Home*, it said. He hesitated.

"I don't want flowers," said Mrs. Wilcox.

Jesse brought her the bag and she asked that he empty the contents on her bed. She took a container of pills but lacked the strength to open it. Standing on his good leg, Jesse reached over to unscrew the cap, and then emptied the vial into her shaking hand. *This is what she wants,* he thought. But his heart that was so full of purpose and vengeance only a moment ago was now teeming with emotions that he didn't understand. When Mrs. Wilcox went to swallow the pills, Jesse gently laid his left crutch on her arm to prevent her from raising it. "Please," he begged, leaning forward and wrapping her hand in his. "Let me get you some water."

Betty Wilcox nodded.

Jesse instead pushed the call button on her headboard with the tip of the crutch, then seated himself on her bed.

"Doctor," she said. "Can I swallow these?" Minutes passed and still Jesse sat there, holding her hand in his. He listened for footsteps but only heard the drone of the machinery she was hooked up to, and her short, rhythmic breaths.

"It's not a good idea, Mrs. Wilcox," said Jesse finally.

A tall nurse who he didn't recognize walked into the room. "What are you doing here?" she said. "And where did you get that coat?"

"Marie said that—"

"Marie doesn't work this shift," said the nurse. "Take it off. Now."

"Look—" Jesse said and he opened his trembling hand to show the nurse Mrs. Wilcox's, still clenching the pills.

"Did she swallow any?"

"No," said Jesse.

The nurse looked closely at the pills, took them from Mrs. Wilcox—who offered no resistance—then raised the bed and checked her vital signs.

Jesse laid the white coat on the chair. Marie had made him feel like a superhero when he wore it. *Chief of Operations*, he thought. *What does that even mean?* He glanced at Mrs. Wilcox. Before leaving the room, with the nurse's back to him, he took a rose from the sill.

He met his mother coming down the hall, and gave her the flower.

"Where did you get it?" she said, pleased.

"Mrs. Wilcox."

"Oh! Did I miss her?"

"No, she's here. Sick."

"And she wanted me to have this?" Jesse was silent. "*Hijo?*"

"I thought I wanted something from her," Jesse said.

"Then you'll have to give it back."

They turned to Mrs. Wilcox's room, but the door was closed. Sarita laid the rose on a stand outside it. She gave Jesse a pen. On a paper toweling he wrote: *Mrs. Wilcox, I took the flower and I'm sorry. I hope you get to go home soon. Jesse.*

"The doctor said that we could leave tomorrow, if the tests are okay," said Sarita. "They'll sew you back up and send us on our way."

"Texas?"

"I found a place for us here. A farm outside Sears Harbor. I think you'll like it. You'll need follow-up appointments and physical therapy. I already scheduled some. I'm going to take classes, and work at the cannery. Your Aunt Teresa in Chicago is loaning us the money to buy a car."

Jesse didn't sleep well that night. When a nurse entered his room in the wee hours of the morning to ask if he was alright, he did not look her in the face. *I'm fine*, he said.

At daybreak they wheeled him onto the elevator and into a different wing. The doctor had determined there was no nerve damage or infection, and closed the remainder of the wound. After breakfast Sarita packed up the few things from his room. They were waiting for their final instructions when Amber—the nurse who had confronted Jesse in Mrs. Wilcox's room—brought a wheelchair, explaining that hospital policy required one at every patient's discharge. And no, he couldn't keep it, only the crutches until his mother arranged for his own. Amber then asked them to follow her down the hall.

"Is this about the insurance?" Sarita asked. Amber said only, "You'll see." When she opened an unmarked door past the nurses' station, a roomful of hospital staff stood up to applaud Jesse. Marie presented him a cake in the shape of a football with blue and silver frosting. Dallas Cowboy colors.

"For our young hero," announced Amber. "You likely saved a patient's life."

Sarita, beaming, looked at Jesse, who burst into tears and quickly wheeled himself out of the room, thanking God that the door had been propped open.

Sarita found him minutes later down the corridor looking out the window over the duck pond. "Jesse—" She put a hand on his still heaving shoulder.

"Mrs. Wilcox told me she wanted to end her life," Jesse said, not turning around, catching his breath between sobs. "And I wanted to help her do that."

The two watched a young boy on the hospital grounds jerk his arm skyward. They saw a stone launch high in the air that in a blink of an eye flitted across their window, like a birdwing. The bright stone plunged downward, breaking the smooth surface of the pond, the ripples reaching the marshy grass some yards away. Sarita pulled Jesse close.

Pleased To Meet You

David Medina

I'm in the wrong place at the wrong time, and so help me, I'm going to do whatever it takes to get out of this mess if it's the last thing I do. I should be in Washington, DC, interviewing presidents, buttonholing congressmen, chasing down the next Watergate scandal. I've earned it after sixteen years of busting my hump for the *Examiner*. I did tours on the night shift, the police beat, the court beat, Bronx Borough Hall, Queens Borough Hall, City Hall, and most recently, the education beat, where I caught a school superintendent falsifying test scores and got him fired. Washington is the logical next step up for me. It's about time I moved into a beat, where everything I write has broad implications.

If I were as good at playing politics as I am at covering it, I'd be there already. I'm not, unfortunately. I talk a good game. But, I don't complain. I don't make demands. I don't threaten and I don't have the guts to trade on favors. I know my place. I do my job better than most anyone else at this paper and I expect to be rewarded accordingly. I grew up in Bushwick. Writing for the *Examiner* surpasses anything that I imagined myself doing at this stage of my life. I'm eternally grateful for the opportunity, even as the editors keep fucking me out of the better assignments.

At least, that's what I tell myself as I snake through the crowd in the marbled atrium of the Manhattan Criminal Courts Building, where the *Examiner* has stationed me as an alternative to the Washington bureau. I should have seen it coming. The atrium resembles Grand Central Station at rush hour, a palatial open space whose architectural grandeur is lost on the multitude of well-dressed lawyers with dueling soft leather satchels; beefy police officers, popping out of their uniforms; bail bondsmen, sniffing about like sewer rats; and the raggedy collection of witnesses, crime victims, and grieving family members who flood this place on a daily basis. The junior prosecutors gather here to run up their tally of guilty pleas, and the defense attorneys come to get their clients off with little or no prison time. They greet each other, not as adversaries but as collaborators. Except for major crimes, like murder, rape, and armed robbery, where the only possible outcomes are freedom or an eternity in jail, both sides want to avoid costly, time-consuming trials. So they swap guilty pleas to reduced charges for lower sentences, then they get a judge to bless each transaction and everybody walks away as though they've won something. Of course, there's always that one idiot in a thousand who rejects the plea offer on the mistaken notion that he can b-s a trial jury into finding him innocent. But generally speaking, the haggling is designed to keep the traffic of cases flowing and prevent systemwide gridlock.

Gridlock occurs when the volume of cases increases faster than the prosecutors' ability to keep pace with it. And when gridlock occurs, prosecutors suddenly become incredibly lenient in an effort to shrink the list back to a manageable size. Those who work in the courthouse— the cleaning crew, the secretaries, the clerks, the stenographers, the security detail, even the judges—refer to those exceptional moments among themselves as "get-out-of-jail free" days. Everyone in the building walks around with the same wily grin that you see at Belmont Race Track when word spreads that a particular race has been fixed in favor of a particular horse. If you're caught stealing a car on such a day, you have an excellent chance of bargaining down the felony possession of stolen property charge to a misdemeanor, such as unlicensed operation of a stolen vehicle, and off you'd go on your own recognizance with only a modest fine to pay.

"Are you pleading guilty voluntarily?" the judges ask each defendant, before signing off on their deal, as if they didn't already know the answer.

"Oh, yes, your honor."

Here and there, as I listen in on plea negotiations, I pick up the usual smidgens of idle chatter about the aggravations of placing kids in private pre-school, golf handicaps, and the unsatisfying state of the stock market. If I didn't already know my way around this dump, I'd be less distressed about being here. I sensed that something was up, when my city editor, Dan O'Brien, summoned me to his office last week for a chat. He had never done that before. Hank Bassett, the editor-in-chief, is typically the one who makes a big show of announcing promotions in front of the entire news staff. That's when O'Brien told me I was going back to covering criminal court. The fat blimp actually tried to make the transfer sound like a step up—as though the paper was sending me on a special secret mission.

"This could be a big opportunity for you," he said in a hushed conspiratorial voice. "We hear that this new DA plans to run for the Senate in two years. Hank and I talked it over and decided that we need a reporter with your skills there to keep an eye on him."

Editors always say crap like that when they screw you.

"Gee, Dan, I kind of had my eye on the White House correspondent's job. It's been vacant for weeks. Why can't I go there?"

"The Washington bureau isn't ready for you yet."

"What do you mean?"

"Frank, it's not always the best reporter that gets the promotion. It's the one that serves our needs at the moment; and, right now, we need you in the courthouse."

"What's the matter? Are the Washington guys afraid I might show them up?"

"Noooo. But the job requires a team player who will look out for the paper's interests, and as we both know, you tend to go rogue on us from time to time. We don't think Washington is the right place for you yet. You'll get your chance one day."

"When, Dan? I'm here sixteen years already."

"Drop it, Frank. Nothing you say is going to change the decision. So why don't you just play the hand that's been dealt you and be thankful you have a job."

Until that moment, I never seriously considered the limits to my career at the *Examiner*. I have joked from time to time about how decades from now when I'm old and feeble the powers-that-be at the paper will put me out to pasture on the obituary desk or at some other dead-end beat where old and feeble reporters go to die. It startles me to think now that my banishment to the courthouse is the *Examiner*'s way of telling me without warning that I've hit my limit.

"Frank, are you okay?"

"Okay?" I said, as if awakening from a trance. "I really don't know, Dan. Am I?"

"Tell you what, take the rest of the week off and do whatever it is you do to relax and take your mind off the job. You'll get over it by Monday."

I dragged myself out of the newsroom, head slung low, avoiding eye contact as I passed the reporters, who were peering solemnly at me over their desktop computers. I went home; prayed for O'Brien and Bassett to be sucked into a running wood chipper; I cried over my fate and rammed my fist through the bathroom mirror, then cried some more; and here I am, headed for my first meeting with interim district attorney, John Kettering III, freshly plucked out of Greenwich, Connecticut, by Gov. George Sutton to fill in for the recently deceased

Victor Batista. I ride the courthouse elevator to the eleventh floor and enter a passageway that leads to the reception area of Kettering's office in an adjoining building. A third adjoining building, the twelve-story Manhattan Detention Center (also known as "The Tombs") sits on the opposite side of the courthouse, allowing for the easy transfer of prisoners from their jail cells to the courtrooms by way of another series of connecting passageways. The stale odor of ancient mahogany wall panels vaults into my nasal passages as I enter the reception area to Kettering's office. Some things never change. I feel like a man who has been forced to move back in with his parents after squandering all his money.

As prosecutors go, Kettering is no Frank Hogan or Robert Morgenthau. Rumor has it that he's never even been inside a courtroom. He's a pure-bred corporate attorney from an upper-crust family that put a ton of money into Gov. Sutton's last reelection campaign, which gives his appointment, however temporary, at least the appearance of impropriety. Yet, a glowing editorial in the *Examiner* said the governor was "wise" to select someone with no previous ties to the city's political establishment as Batista's short-term replacement.

There's a woman in black, seated at the desk that guards Kettering's office door. She's a bit on the plus side, late twenties to early thirties, with the right curves in the right places. Her cheery eyelashes dance like butterfly wings and there's a gold crucifix sunning itself on the left breast that's snow-coning over her neckline. A large pair of gold hoop earrings peek out from behind her black satin waterfall of hair. She keeps a little flag of Puerto Rico in her pencil cup. A framed photo of her with a lookalike toddler at her side stands next to the cup. I see no photos of her with a man and she's not wearing a wedding ring. She reminds me of the party girls I hungered for as a kid in Bushwick. "Girls like that are no good," my mother would say. "If you want to get out of this stinking place, stay away from them. Get your education." I picture this woman behind the desk with a GED, perhaps a year of community college, and a seemingly endless string of temp jobs before finally landing a full-time government position with health benefits that she's trying hard not to lose for the sake of that kid in the photo.

"You must be Mr. Palomar from the *Examiner*."

"Rumor has it," I say. "And you are?"

"Angie, Angie Camacho."

"It's a pleasure to meet you, Angie."

Angie picks up the receiver on her desk phone and informs "District Attorney Kettering" on the other side of the wall behind her that I have arrived. She pauses briefly to listen, then in a surprisingly snobbish tone she says, "District Attorney Kettering asks that you kindly have a seat. He'll be ready for you in a minute or so." She's obviously a new hire, perhaps repeating Kettering's exact words. Her annoying way of calling him "District Attorney Kettering," as if she were saying "His Highness," adds to my frustration with this new assignment. Imagine having to listen to that every day. Then there's the waiting. A "minute or so" turns to five, which turns into ten. I kill time by counting the pimples on the alternating green and beige porcelain tiles at my feet. A short alcove to my right leads to an oak door with the words "District Attorney John D. Kettering III" painted in gold leaf on a frosted glass pane.

"Is that your son in the photo?" I ask Angie.

"Yep, that's my little man, Ricky."

"How old is he?"

"He just turned five."

"Is he in school yet?"

"Preschool. I pick him up at my mother's place after work. You got kids?"

"I have a girl, Veronica. She's ten."

"Divorced?" It occurs to me that I'm not wearing a wedding ring either.

"Uh-huh. Veronica lives with her mother."

Angie's desk phone buzzes.

"District Attorney Kettering will see you now."

"Thank you, Angie."

The door opens before my fingers touch the brass knob and there's Kettering in a tailored navy pinstripe and flawlessly tousled brown hair with a touch of grey at the temples. He neither shakes my hand nor looks me in the eyes. He waves me in with a sweep of this arm.

"Pleased to meet you, Frank."

I sense an impatience to check me off his to-do list and move on to more important matters.

"Pleased to meet you too."

I cross the threshold and suddenly I'm in a wonderland of photographs, canvass paintings, and sculptures, all neatly mounted over waist-high bookcases stacked with law books. My layman's grasp of fine art only recognizes the Andy Warhol and Jackson Pollock paintings, and a two-foot-high wooden abstract by Louise Nevelson, on which a vintage flannel New York Yankees baseball cap hangs irreverently. The floor space is divided into quadrants. A carved antique mahogany desk with a high-backed leather office chair occupies the furthest corner to my right. A fifteen-foot-long teak conference table with matching chairs stretches out from my immediate right. And a pair of bright yellow love seats mirror each other across the two quadrants to my left. Gauzy white panel curtains cover the four arched windows on the far wall, letting in daylight while masking the view of The Tombs. I half expect the furnishings to jump up and do a Walt Disney musical number. For someone who's projected to be here no more than eighteen months, Kettering wasted no time in making himself at home.

He motions me to sit on the sofa that faces a wall of 8 x10-inch photographs of him posing with very important people in ways that suggest he hangs out with them on a regular basis. Every politician I know keeps an office photo gallery. The galleries reveal as much about the politician as they do about how he or she wants to be perceived. The man-of-the-people types prefer photos of themselves surrounded by constituent groups such as the local seniors' club members on bingo night or a congregation of black Baptist churchgoers on a Sunday morning. Others display themselves behind a series of podiums, delivering inspirational speeches. Then there are those who want to be seen in the company of other politicians of equal or higher rank to show that they've got juice. But the photos they all crave the most are the ones of them dedicating a new building, any building, because it's the only concrete proof that they've accomplished anything while in office.

Kettering sits across from me on the opposite sofa with his back to the gallery. I can't resist peeking past his shoulder to measure where he falls in the spectrum. I see Kettering with Nelson Mandela, with Roger Federer and Serena Williams. Kettering with Justin Trudeau. Kettering as a boy on Muhammad Ali's knee. Kettering with Gloria Steinem. With Oprah. With Jane Fonda. And—as if I needed any more grief today—Kettering with his arm draped over the shoulders of Byron Lloyd, the publisher of the *Examiner*, like a pair of old college chums.

I pretend not to notice the Lloyd photo. I doubt Kettering placed it there for my benefit. It's easy to see how he and Lloyd might travel in the same social circles. Lloyd inherited the paper from his father, who inherited it from his grandfather, who inherited the paper from his great-grandfather about one hundred years ago. Kettering leans back on the sofa and swings one lanky leg over the other, exposing his argyle socks and a pair of raisin-colored loafers with little tassels on the vamps.

"The floor is yours, Frank. What do you want to discuss?"

"I just wanted to introduce myself, since it seems we're going to be interacting a lot for the foreseeable future." I try to sound as though I'm tickled to be here again.

"That's it? No trick questions?" Kettering grins as he rocks his raised leg restlessly.

I grit my teeth and smile. If I had balls, I would ask him about the black girl from New Haven that his parents paid off to abort his baby back when he attended Yale Law. Byron Lloyd's smiling face warns me that I better not. Officially, the abortion never happened. Although I have it on good authority that the girl signed a confidentiality agreement allowing the family lawyer to witness the procedure before handing her the check.

"No trick questions," I say.

I'm here to make nice. So I sit there, lunged forward, in a rumpled khaki suit from JCPenney's and day-old stubble on my face, babbling through my escape from the badlands of Bushwick—single mother, public school, welfare, gangs, drugs, and a few lucky breaks—to the comforting arms of the *New York Examiner*, along with a short review of major stories I wrote that he might be old enough to remember. I have discovered that people of Kettering's pedigree love it when common homo sapiens like me overcome adversity and rise above our level. They can express sympathy, while clinging to the belief that they're a morally superior species. When I'm done with my spiel, I fully expect Kettering to proudly stick out his chest and remark how wonderful it is that we live in the land of opportunity, rather than compliment me on my personal achievements. To my surprise, his eyes glaze over. I'm clearly not the first drudge that has ever tried to impress him with my struggles.

"I'm sorry. Am I boring you?"

"No, not at all," he says. Then, out of nowhere, he adds, "I'm just curious as to why you haven't touched upon the Ramón Valdez case."

The mention of Ray Valdez makes me cringe, and judging from the smug little glint in Kettering's eyes, that's exactly what he wanted to do. The Valdez case is buried so far beneath the landfill of things I'd rather forget that my mind shakes it off sometimes, as though it never happened. Kettering must have been in high school, when I wrote about it. So—as if I don't have enough to worry about already—why is he bringing Valdez up now?

"I'd be more inclined to talk about it if Valdez had gone to jail. But he didn't."

I discovered Valdez years ago while I was on the night shift. cleaning up scraps left over by the dayside reporters and waiting for the mythical next plane to hit the Empire State Building. He was the brains behind a little known Democratic political club in the Bronx, where I found out that people named to high-ranking city jobs, judgeships, and building contracts had quietly delivered hundreds of thousands of dollars in payoffs disguised as party donations. O'Brien and Bassett went so nuts over what I wrote that they enshrined my stories on Page 1. After two weeks of this, the former district attorney announced an investigation and empaneled a grand jury. Our readers ate it up. Valdez became the poster boy for corrupt city government and my star at the *Examiner* was rising. Then a funny thing happened. The grand jury refused to indict Valdez. The prosecution had failed to produce evidence that he had pocketed any of the money. As far as the grand jury was concerned, the payoffs were lawful political contributions.

Kettering won't let it go.

"Why so bitter? You're not to blame for what the grand jury did."

"Thanks, but I'd rather my name not be associated with the fish that got away." My voice grows increasingly strident. "When you invest that much ink on someone you know in your bones is corrupt, it had better result in a lengthy trial and, preferably, a guilty verdict. It keeps readers glued to the paper for months. Anything less is failure, as far as I'm concerned. What else would you like to know?"

Kettering shakes his head quickly and backs off.

"Good," I say. "Now, would you tell me what exactly Governor Sutton said to you when he approached you about taking this job? It must have been a fascinating conversation."

Kettering smiles. His leg rocks like the handle of an old ground water pump, as his brain formulates a response. "Not at all," he says. "The governor called me up one day and asked if I would like to be district attorney for eighteen months. I thought about it and said yes. I figured—Why not?—putting bad people away could be fun." He shakes his fists like a timid child pretending to be a boxer. "Besides, it gives me something noteworthy to be remembered for."

"Just like that? Hi, John, would you like to be district attorney?"

"More or less."

"Did your lack of experience come up at all?"

"No. Why would it? I'm only here a short while, and we have a perfectly capable staff of attorneys here to advise me on the legal stuff."

"So what do you plan to do when you're finished here? Run for office? Go back to drawing up corporate contracts?"

The leg swings even higher. The glint in his eye reappears.

"I have no idea, but I'm open to any and all possibilities."

I don't buy any of it. But I hesitate to press him further, while Byron Lloyd is watching. I remind myself that I'm here to make nice. There'll be plenty of time to grill him later. After a painfully long silence that may have revealed my feelings on the matter, Kettering changes the subject.

"So how is this interaction between you and I supposed to work, Frank?"

"It depends. It can either be hostile or cooperative. Ideally, I would have direct access to you by cell phone at any time day or night for when I need answers in a hurry and can't get them from your deputies."

"What if I don't want to be identified as your source for this information?"

"Simple. You tell me everything you know off the record. Then you point me toward a secondary source or any paper document that confirms what you say without my having to name you in my story. Just don't lie or withhold information. I'll find out eventually."

Kettering stares me down grimly.

"And what happens if there's nothing to support what I tell you?"

If there's no backup source you're probably lying, I want to say.

"Then you'll have to really persuade me that I can't confirm the information elsewhere before I credit it to Mr. Anonymous. Almost everything we do leaves a trail of some sort. It's just a matter of finding it."

Kettering rubs his forehead and mulls over what I've told him.

"Sounds acceptable," he says. And with that, he pulls a business card from his breast pocket and hands it to me. "There's my cell number."

He seems to want to keep things friendly. I rise to shake his hand and get the hell out of there before he changes his mind about working with me.

"Thank you. I won't take up any more of your time."

Kettering, still pondering, looks down at my outstretched hand and ignores it. Anyone would think I was diseased. Thank goodness I no longer let things like that bother me.

"One last thing," His eyebrows suddenly scrunch with concern. He gestures me to sit down again. "Let me see how I can phrase this," he says. "On a purely hypothetical basis, how do you think the city would react if Mr. Valdez were investigated and charged again?"

"Charged with what?"

"Oh, I don't know, I was speaking hypothetically. I'm sure we can find something."

Three chilling thoughts converge in my head: that Kettering is a bit too hung up on Valdez, that he's remarkably unaware of Valdez's power, and that the last thing I need right now is to get caught up in reliving the past.

"Look," I say. "Most people in the city are okay with Valdez being shady. He's *supposed* to be shady. He's a political boss. His job is to pull strings for people. So, to answer your question, charging him with a crime will not be well received, even by people who think he's guilty. You'd be hard pressed to find twelve jurors who either don't owe him a favor or aren't related to someone who does. Welcome to New York."

Kettering closes his eyes and takes a deep meditational breath, then pastes on a weary smile.

"As I said, I was speaking hypothetically. Please, don't read anything into it."

"Fine. Are we done?"

He rises. Another sweep of his arm invites me to leave.

"It's been a pleasure meeting you, Frank."

On my way out, I notice that Angie has the wary-eyed look of someone who expects to be horsewhipped at any moment. I turn back to whisper into Kettering's ear: "Would you do me a favor and tell this young lady—what's her name again?"

"Angie."

"—Angie. Would you please tell Angie here that it's okay to call you 'Mr. Kettering,' instead of District Attorney Kettering all the time? It makes you seem unapproachable."

Kettering thinks about it a moment.

"Point well taken."

I manage to make it back to the atrium, dizzied and gasping for air, as if I'd spent the last hour under water. I steady myself against the railing of a winding marble staircase that leads to a row of shabby offices for a variety of probation, social service, drug rehab, and anger management programs that freed defendants must register with as a condition of their plea deals. It sickens me to think that a week ago I was cruising the internet for DC-area apartment rentals in my price range, only to find myself back where I started, babysitting a fill-in district attorney with no talent for the job.

I rush out of the courthouse and vanish into the crush of lunchtime pedestrians headed toward Chinatown. I duck behind a Dumpster reeking of rotten seafood in the alley next to Chengdu's Restaurant on Mott Street to speed dial a call that I don't want overheard.

"If it isn't the Honorable Frank Palomar. To what do I owe the privilege of this overdue telephone call after—what—a year and a half?"

"Hi, Ray. How are you and the family?"

"Good. But that's not why you called. What's up?"

"You and I need to have a private conversation as soon as possible."

"What about?"

"I'll tell you when I get there."

I hear a long sigh that sounds like the wheeze of a subway train after it grinds to a halt.

"Tuesday, ten thirty. The usual place."

"See you then."

The Lunatic, The Lover, and The Lawyer

David Bontumasi

Most movie stars have had plastic surgery, I'm sure of it, even the young ones. They have that work done and still they need to sit in a makeup chair for hours each morning, so they can look perfect on film. That's a fact. Still, after the surgery and the makeup, they need to be photographed from their good side and in the right light. So, at the end of the day, it ends up being about the magic of certain angles. You see, no matter what you think, absolutely nothing you see on a movie screen is real.

I'm not an actress, I'm just a regular person, so I can say all that, but you don't have to be in the movies to have people like you. I visit people when I make claims visits for the insurance company I work for and I make people happy in my work too. Isn't that just as good? And that's real life. That's real-life happiness. I make them smile and I'm a normal person. But what is happiness, really? The poets tell you that being happy and falling in love is a fleeting proposition, anyway.

We hadn't been out in months and I begged Michael, my fabulous husband of nineteen years, to go see a movie. We both needed a break. Do something, away from the TV and our books, and escape the confines of our modest but suffocating Victorian with the dated furniture, mounds of clutter, and peeling plaster. Sure, we live in a nice town, but our house is the smallest one on the block, our lawn has a lot of brown patches. I thought when you married a lawyer, you'd live the good life, you'd be comfortable, you'd have money to travel and do things, but we're definitely not well off. We hate flying and we don't get away on the weekends much anymore, so a trip to the movie theater seemed like a mini-vacation. To me, anyway. Michael's a litigation lawyer at Orrington, Crane & Associates, a small firm in the city, and where the money goes is beyond me. I don't care about the money, though, I never have. All I ever wanted was to have a comfortable marriage with Michael, like my parents had, and have a good life.

It was in high school that I really fell in love with literature. Maybe it was because of Mr. Berry in tenth grade, I'm sure it was, since everybody had a crush on him, even the boys. He wore cardigans with turtlenecks underneath and he'd push the sleeves up to his elbows as he sat on the corner of his desk, one leg swinging. He was so convincing, discussing the characters, and the plot twists. I read *Anna Karenina* in his class and remembered liking it. It was hard not to love the classics, listening to Mr. Berry talk, moving his arms and pushing up his glasses. He was smart and very handsome, a real-life cross between Mr. Darby and Dean Moriarty.

Michael loves thrillers, but I love the classics. Shakespeare—oh, how I loved MIDSUMMER'S NIGHT DREAM and the sonnets—Tolstoy, James Joyce, and Brontë, Eliot and Dickinson. I wished I could write like them, I wished I could make people happy like they all made me. I loved the plots and the characters, and I loved getting lost in the romance of the words, strung together before me like endless rolling waves on a shoreline.

I usually try to stay away from film adaptations as they are never, ever as good as the book, but I heard that they made a new movie of *Anna Karenina* and it was playing at the multiplex near us, so I suggested it to Michael. I knew he wouldn't like it, but it was a chance to get out, and it made me think of Mr. Barry and everything I loved. It ended up being the biggest mistake of my life.

When we got back in the car, Michael said the film was "alright." That's what he said. He shrugged his shoulders and said, "It was alright," as he started up the car. That reaction was what I expected, I thought to myself, that's all I could ask for. Michael's smart, but he could be a little dense sometimes and miss the point of any great story unless it hit him in the noggin. I gathered my coat against my chest and said that I liked it. Zoe Robeson was the actress who played Anna and she was good and the actor who played Karenin was very good looking but awfully stiff, I told Michael. I still loved the story. I liked the pace and thought the cinematography was lovely, especially the scene at the station where she steps in front of the train, with all the fog and rain. That's what I told him, like I was a movie critic or something.

For days afterward, Michael seemed down. He was quieter than normal, and he kept frowning, like he was vexed with a case at work and could not, for the life of him, figure it out. I thought maybe he was mad at me, but it didn't make sense. I hadn't done anything. I asked him if he was okay and he just nodded. On Thursday night, a full four days later, Michael got home from work and put his leather briefcase on the dining-room table. He never does that, he usually sets it on the floor, by the shoe mat near the front door. He walked into the kitchen and looked at the floor tiles for a few seconds before he raised his head.

"Avery, can we talk?"

Just from that, I could tell it was serious. He never calls me "Avery"; he usually calls me Avy.

"Okay," I said and wiped my hands on the towel and turned towards him. His face was ashen. "Is everything okay? Did they let you go?"

"No," he shook his head.

He cleared his throat and loosened his tie. "This is going to be hard."

"What's wrong?"

"Something happened."

"What happened?" I couldn't take it. "Did you get into a car accident? What happened?"

"I've fallen in love."

He said the words, those four words, and everything stopped. Everything in my world stopped. Those four words floated above his head, like a puff of thick smoke. They hovered in the air, formless but pregnant with intent, slowly inching their way to me. I couldn't say anything, really, I couldn't breathe. I closed my eyes and let those four engorged words land on me, like a wet bag bursting open and revealing scores of spiders, shuttering and twittering over me in all directions, making my skin crawl. Michael faded away behind a foggy glaze, and I must have looked ridiculous, standing there, frozen, mouth slung open, eyes glistening as I waited for him to come back into view. I wanted a clearer Michael to stand in front of me, one with better answers. Michael was a sluggish man, a little frumpy, slow and methodical; that's how my sister talked about him, but he was a good person, he meant well. I never would have thought he could've said something like that or that he would even think that. I couldn't fathom that he could say those words out loud to me.

"I didn't mean for it to happen, and really, it makes no sense at all, I know that. I mean, I'm not stupid. I can see how this must look, but it is what it is, and I have to face it. We just have to accept that."

How quickly your life changes in a heartbeat, a whisper, the blink of an eye, from one frame on a roll of film cascading to the next.

"Accept what? What are you talking about? Don't tell me to accept it." I put the dishtowel on the counter. "Are we getting a divorce? Are you saying we're getting a divorce? Just like that?"

I couldn't believe I said that word, that all of this was happening. Suddenly, I realized we were now one of those couples that, in the past, we would've shaken our heads at and said to each other, with a smile, "At least that's not us."

"Yes, I would think so," he said. "I think it's only fair to you. And to me, of course."

"You've fallen in love with some other woman?"

He seemed to wince at the question, so I altered the wording. "Or is it a man? Are you in love with a man?"

"No, no, don't be crazy, no, it's not like that."

"Then what's it like, Michael? What's going on? Tell me what it's like."

"I've fallen in love with someone else and I think we should get a divorce. Before I said anything to you, I needed to make sure of my feelings and I had to be sure of the next steps, of what needs to be done. I know this is crazy, but I had to be sure. If I had fallen in love—and I have—I wanted to be fair and to be realistic. I thought a lot about it and I really want to be fair."

"Yeah, you said that already. How very thoughtful of you. I don't even know what you're talking about. How is this fair? How is any of this fair? How long has this been going on?"

"Not long. I mean, well, I wanted you to know as soon as I was sure. I didn't want to hide it."

I walked past him and sat on a chair in the dining room. My legs felt rubbery and my stomach queasy. "Who is it? No, don't tell me, I don't want to know. Just tell me, is she younger than me? She's really young, isn't she? No, don't tell me that. I don't want to know." Suddenly my head began to throb. "Oh God, is it someone I know?" Michael shook his head. I pushed my hands against my temples as the batch of spiders began to make their way over my skin, the tickly, soft scuttering of their legs pinning a great weight beneath them. I felt itchy and antsy and very, very sick, all over, all at once. "God damn you, Michael, God damn you!"

"I'm sorry, Avery, I really am."

"Oh, shut up."

I wanted Michael to stop talking, but at the same time, I wanted to know so much more, I wanted him to tell me things, everything in his heart. I had so many questions but the answers, I knew, I'd never get from Michael.

"I didn't want to hurt you, but sometimes things happen and you can't plan for them. I see this kind of thing happening all around—we both have—the craziest things happen. You can't foresee them. You can only accept them. You have to realize that fate is what it is, and you have to go with it. Both of us do."

He was reasoning this out, methodically, like he always did, like a legal summation, but I wanted more of his emotions, I needed more.

"It's fate? Is that what this is, some kind of once-in-a-lifetime miracle?" He didn't say anything. "Is that right, Michael? The stars aligned for you and you finally found your soulmate? Your true love? Oh, how lucky for you."

"Yes. I didn't want to say that out loud, but yes, I think I have. I've been thinking about that and I think I've found something. I mean, I know I have. I think I'm happy."

"What are you talking about? You're happy? What the devil are you talking about? What do you know about it?"

He stood next to the dining-room table, his arms dangling at his side.

He didn't look happy: He looked uncomfortable, he looked miserable, he looked like he hadn't slept in days, a spare tire hanging loosely around his midsection, his skin pasty, his thin hair pushed tightly across his forehead. Through the middle-aged veneer, something in him seemed vulnerable, like a schoolboy standing in a doorway of a new classroom at midterm. His eyes looked sad, his brows pinched in fear. He didn't know which way to go. As much as I wanted to hit him as hard as I have ever wanted to hit anyone, I also wanted to pull him back from that doorway, hug him, assure him that he didn't need to do this to make himself feel better. We could work on it. It would pass. He was still my Michael and I was still his Avy. There was no one else.

"Who is this person? Who is this woman?"

"This is the really hard part," he said and scratched at his cheek.

"Oh God. Who?"

"Well, it's going to seem strange, but it really makes all the sense in the world."

"I feel sick. Is it someone I know?"

Michael stared at me.

"I'm waiting."

"Zoe Robeson."

"Who?"

"Zoe Robeson."

"Zoe Robeson? Is that what you said? Zoe Robeson, the actress?" I couldn't believe what he just said. "Zoe Robeson? I really don't understand anything that's happening right now. Do you know Zoe Robeson? Zoe Robeson, the actress? Who probably lives in Hollywood, a million miles away from our house in Middleton?"

"She has a house on Long Island too."

"How do you know that?"

"I looked it up."

"You don't know Zoe Robeson, Michael, she doesn't know you. Are you joking about this?" I shook my head and began to laugh. But I really couldn't laugh, so it came out like a muffled cough. "I can't believe this. You have a schoolboy crush on a movie actress young enough to be your daughter, the daughter you never had, and you want to throw away our marriage on that? We're supposed to celebrate our twentieth anniversary next year, or did you forget that? Jesus, Michael, what are you thinking? And you're okay, throwing all that away, pushing it aside for the movie star, Zoe Robeson, someone you don't even know? Have you seen any of her films before the one we saw the other night?"

He shook his head.

"Zoe Robeson is an actress, Michael. You know that, right? You know she's really not Anna Karenina? She didn't really get hit by a train. She doesn't need you to save her."

"Yes, of course I know that."

"So, let me get this straight. You have a crush on an actress playing a role, a role in a movie, which is based on a novel by Tolstoy? I mean, are you serious? Have you lost your mind?"

Michael tightened his lips and stood up straight, better to deflect my responses.

"She's an actress, Michael, one you will never, ever in your wildest dreams, never actually meet, yet alone have a romantic relationship with. What do you plan to do—leave me and go live at the movie theater, watching her movies over and over at every showing? Jesus.

"She's an actress. And not a very good one. I think you can agree with me on that. You saw her once on a big movie screen. She was playing a role, and she got paid to say those lines. The character and the words are not even her words, do you know that? If you think about it, Michael, if you really think about it, you really have a crush on Tolstoy. You've actually fallen in love with Leo Tolstoy. Your true love is a Russian writer from two hundred years ago, with a stern brow and large crinkly white beard. That's your soulmate, Michael, that's who you really fell in love with. Let that sink in for a while."

I buried my head in my hands and squished the skin of my cheeks into my cheekbones.

Michael rested the tip of his fingers on the table, close enough to finger-walk over to my bent arm, but he didn't touch me. He cleared his throat.

"You're wrong, Avery. I didn't fall in love with Tolstoy. That's ridiculous. I fell in love with a woman, who just happens to be a famous actress. Love is crazy like that; I know that now. What you don't think is possible is suddenly possible, if you fight for it. I know it was the character she was playing, I'm not stupid, but I could see the struggle in her eyes. It was her eyes. It was the character, but it was her. It was real. I connected with that. I know it's crazy, but I know what I'm doing."

I needed for him to stop talking for a bit. Or forever. I covered my ears. I couldn't think, I couldn't feel anything, I couldn't begin to do anything except try to move very slowly and ease myself out from under the layer of spiders crawling all over my body, one by one. Every part of me hurt to think of Michael like this, gone off the deep end, under a spell of fantasy overtaking reality, and throwing our relationship away with it. Bathed in the silence, our bodies were so close, almost touching, yet Michael seemed like a negative version of his old self. I wanted to go back, to just a day ago, a week ago. I missed our lives, our marriage; I missed Michael's laugh, and it seemed so wrong that he would toss away everything with me so easily, without a second thought.

He slept on the couch that night and then moved out the next day. Just like that. On Friday, five days after we saw that stupid movie, he was gone. He left quietly and without saying good-bye to our Labrador, Willie, named for William Shakespeare. Within a week, he had quit his job and moved to California. He called me from the road or somewhere and told me that.

"I just wanted you to know. Where I was, and what's happening."

"Why, Michael? What do I care? You closed the door on your life here, forgot it ever happened, quit your job. What did they say at work? What did Orrington say when you told him you were leaving? Did he punch you? Did he hit you?"

"No, I didn't get into it. I didn't want them to know everything. I told them I had a different opportunity, that I had to oversee a special project."

"A different opportunity? Oh, that's perfect. You should have told him that your special project was to be the President of Fantasyland. But instead you made it nice and clean, huh, Michael? Of course."

"You're still angry, that makes—"

"Yeah, probably best not to burn any bridges, Michael. You may need all the people you've thrown away on a whim, all the people you've just pushed aside."

"It's not a whim, Avery."

"Did you realize you didn't even say good-bye to Willie? He mopes around the house. He still thinks you're going to walk him each morning and each night. And he growls when I feed him."

It hurt that he was calling me Avery now. It was like I didn't exist anymore as a person, that I had been reduced to my birth name imprinted on a piece of paper.

"I wanted to call and say I was sorry about all this. I wanted to tell you that I'm really—"

"Next time you want to release some guilt, don't call Avery, call Zoe Robeson, okay? Good luck with that, Michael," I said and hung up the phone.

Life without Michael, after so long, was strange. We hadn't really ever been apart in all our years together. A night here or there, but nothing more than that. This felt empty and deathly and permanent. I wondered if he felt that way too. I had Willie, but he was mostly Michael's dog before, so I was alone, really alone. I hadn't really been alone before, not like that. I would sit in the living room and stare at the waves in the cushion fabric where he used to sit. I wondered when it was that he last sat there. I sat in the kitchen and looked at the wall behind Michael's chair, the space that I didn't see before because he was sitting there. All the rooms in the house were empty. Every room I entered now knew only my movements and rhythms. I did everything I used to do before, but somehow I had a lot more time. I began to read again, Shakespeare and Poe and Tolstoy and Chekhov. I also read Stephen King, and Sue Grafton. The evenings dragged on; the nights lingered. Everything was quiet, so quiet, every thought was amplified in my brain, like a fuzzy announcement at a train terminal. It gave me time to clean the house: I got rid of the piles, threw a bunch of stuff away, most of it without a second glance. I cleaned everything off the dining-room table and the coffee table, for the first time, in what seemed like years. I had direction, but at the same time, I was also immobile. I could only move in circles, so I always ended up where I started. I moved through each day feeling as if I was on the verge of something or waiting for something else to happen. I just didn't know what, but I kept waiting. Waiting. I wasn't sure what I was waiting for—a knock on the door, a phone call, a familiar face or a voice, a smell, anything. I waited to see Michael again, for him to call and tell me how wrong he was and beg me to take him back. I waited and waited, and then the waiting turned into a constant, nagging hum. I waited some more. I longed for him to return, his tail between his legs, saying he'd been foolish, to say that he dove in blindly and was in way over his head. I needed to hear him say he was sorry he hurt me.

How long does it take to try to find a movie star's house, but then realize that there's no way to get past her large wrought-iron gates or wriggle past her bodyguard? Would he ever even catch a glimpse of her? How long would he try? Would he get arrested for bothering her or stalking her? I hoped he wouldn't call me to bail him out, but then, if he did, I could probably be out there the next day. Instead, I just kept waiting. How long would he try before he would give up? How long before he realized how truly delusional he had been?

At first, if people asked, I told them that he was on a business trip, but it soon felt like I was covering up for him. I then started to tell people that Michael left, he went to California to "find himself." I'd shrug my shoulders, their jaw would drop, and they'd bring a hand to the cheek.

There was nothing I could do. "You mean he left? Just like that? Oh, how awful for you."

I'm not sure when I lost him; I don't know when it all went wrong. I remembered that Michael said something one night when we were grocery shopping, maybe six months before. He was standing near the cheeses and he muttered, "There's got to be something more than this." At the time, I thought he was talking about gouda and extra-sharp cheddar, but maybe he meant something else. I tried to go back through old photographs, and dig through my memory for any clues, but I couldn't find anything. I couldn't remember anything else. I expected some clarity, some answers, but everything got cloudier and further away the more I thought about it. Michael had said that he didn't plan on getting a divorce, that all of this "just happened" so maybe there wasn't anything to find. I took some comfort in knowing that maybe things were good before, just like I thought, but in the same breath, I hated him for throwing a good thing aside so quickly. That's what kept coming back to me—how suddenly it all happened. "You have to go with those feelings," he had said that evening, "You just have to go for it."

It was right around the four-month mark that the second big event happened. It was a Saturday, my usual day to run errands. As I walked around the car that morning, I noticed the stick figure family decals—a man, a woman and a dog—on the back windshield that Michael had been so tickled to attach years ago. I'm not sure why I hadn't remembered them before that, but there you have it. I went back into the house and down the stairs to Michael's workbench, came back, and covered the stickers with one large swathe of gray duct tape. I threw the roll of tape into the back and with a smile, slammed the trunk shut. The grocery store was quiet that day and as I headed to the checkout with my cart halfway full, I noticed it. The *National Enquirer* or whatever it was seemed to suddenly come alive, waving to me from the vertical magazine rack. I picked it up. "America's Sweetheart Quits Hollywood!" the headline screamed. There she was walking down the street in Hollywood, dark sweatpants, a yoga mat curled under her arm, smiling full and wide. I picked up the paper and held it in my hands. "Zoe Robeson says that she has made her last film and will now devote her energies to saving the lives of wild dogs."

I looked back at the photograph, her blond hair pushed back in a loose ponytail, her blue eyes, her head tilted back in the sun. And then I saw it. Right over her shoulder, standing a little behind her, just under the *r* and *t* in the headline was Michael. He was blurry in that grainy newsprint, but it was definitely him. He looked serious, thin, in khakis and a button-down shirt. His hair was pushed up and his face had color.

He looked good, he did, like he was on the vacation that we never went on. I smiled. It was nice to see him. He looked like himself but happier. I don't think he had ever been in the newspaper before and now, there he was on the cover of the *National Enquirer*, part of the lead story. It seemed like a weird dream. Maybe it was strange for Michael, too, I have to think so. I pushed some stray hairs around my ears and scanned the photo. The white blurry building in the background, the portion of a palm tree hanging in from the side, and Zoe in her little, tight outfit next to Michael, my Michael, all in the same shot. The oddest thing is that his right hand was near Zoe's left elbow, as if his first two fingers were assisting her, perhaps guiding her away from the paparazzi. He was so close he was almost touching her. I threw the paper on the conveyor belt and checked out.

When I got home, I put the *National Enquirer* on the kitchen table and slid it toward Michael's side. I thought the old Michael should see it. I poured myself some water and sat in my chair and took small sips until my glass was empty.

"Well, there you have it, you did it," I said to Michael and to no one in particular. The old Michael wasn't coming back.

Three hours later, my heart was beating in my throat. I slid my hand into my bag and pressed my palm flush against the cover of the *National Enquirer,* as I stood at the counter and bought a one-way airline ticket for Los Angeles, California.

As we landed, I looked out the small window: The sun was shining over the mountains, and the sky was so big, a deep, rich blue with perfectly shaped white cloud puffs. It was beautiful. Nothing looked real, like it was all in a movie. I hugged my bag to my chest as we taxied to the gate. I'm going for it, Michael, I told myself, I'll be there soon.

WRITING BY HMS COMMUNITY NONPROFIT PARTNERS

Breakthrough Family Ministries

Above & Beyond Family Recovery Center

St. Leonard's MInistries

Birth

Dominique Murray

I had so many false alarms this time I wanted to be sure.
This is it! She's coming. Hopefully!
I was in so much pain, all I could do is.... Breath....... Blow!
My back ached so bad, I wanted something to ease the pain.
Here I was experiencing the pains of child birth.
I eased my way into bed my belly feeling like an oversized watermelon.
I'm careful not to fall.
He was in the next room. My pride wouldn't let me ask him for his help.
He's helped enough! Look At me. Fat and helpless.
I remember being in so much pain I drove to the drug store and purchased a heating pad for my back.
Is she coming!
They say I'm carrying her in my hips and buttocks.
I drove back home, thinking maybe I should just drive to the hospital.
Something told me no. Don't go alone.
Frustrated, fat, and anxious, I wanted something so beautiful to be over.
Inside my room, I relax with a heating pad while playing some music.
This remedy worked up until this point. But this was the breaking point.
It's got to be time!
Baby daddy drove me to the hospital. I arrived and was wheeled to the maternity ward.
All I could think about was the pain.......
The pain getting intense and intense....... breath
The nurse ordered for a stress test. Then she checked to see if I was dilated.
To my advantage it was time! Finally, my miracle is on the way.

No false alarm today!
I screamed for the nurse to give me an epidural.
I was told to sit up straight and don't move.
There I was relieved because the pain was relieved and soon my baby girl will be coming!
Hours later I was just enough centimeters dilated and it's time. The doctor said' now push.
Out she comes as red and bright as beautiful as the sun.
My baby girl!

I Am the Multi-Colored Man: A Dream

Ronald Yokley

One night I had a drink and smoked a joint. I had been feeling good. But it seemed like I had started turning into another man. I wasn't Ron. I began to turn into somebody else.

I looked into the mirror. I was Superman, Batman, the Hulk, Frederick Douglas, Malcolm X, Harold Washington, the first black mayor of the city. Nate Turner. Hitler. George Washington. But weird thing happened when I jumped into water: I turned into Multi-colored Man. I was super-weird black with green hair and a strange suit, green colored face with dark glasses. Imagine George Clinton with tall boots. And I was riding a fish with a cape. And all of the sudden I was riding a snake. But all of the sudden I became myself again. I did not know what happened to me. I had these different personalities. But I became the Multi-colored Man.

Can you imagine a black man becoming that?

Dear Malcolm

Wesley Cooper

Dear Malcolm,

I hope all is well with you. You had just started a new job—very exciting. The last time I saw you I gave you the *Divine* book. I knew it would give you a chuckle.

So much has happened in my life since then. I feel as though I am reaching out from another country—a far-away place. I suppose I really am.

Poems

William Ruzicka

I Don't Remember

I don't remember
A lot of the pain
And suffering in my life

I don't remember
When I started to believe in God
Just know he's out
There watching over
Us all

I don't remember the last time I have been up North
For a pizza burger

I Don't Remember

I've been told
That I need to
Answer my phone

I've been told I'm
A sweet guy

I've been told I'm
A great guy

I've been told I'm
A good friend

I've been told by Darlene I'm
Her king

Poems

Brian Barnetti

I Remember

I remember my best friend Kevin.
I remember our teacher.
I remember us playing football.
I remember Ann.
I remember when she fell and died.
I remember I sang for cookies and milk.
I remember PO5-1313.
I remember Joyce and Donnell.

I Don't Remember

I don't remember when I lost my spinning top.
I don't remember Faye's kids.
I don't remember where I hid my money.
I don't remember being a bully.

Untitled

I don't know what made me hang with the same goofy guys and girls for so long after knowing the stupid acts they do once intoxicated. I took them to the store with me when my care overheated. They were anxious to get going so, while in the gas station, they took the top off the radiator. All I know I saw three guys running so fast away with a trail of liquid! The fluid shot straight out. Assholes!

Poetry

Toni Lang

Untitled

When I was 7-years old, every evening when I came home from school my great-grandfather was sitting by the heater smoking his pipe in his recliner.

Untitled

In my childhood home the smells that I smell were my mom's perfume and my grandmom's cooking. I hear the television. I hear my grandma and my great grandmom sitting at the kitchen table talking and eating breakfast, my great grandmom perking her coffee. I love the smell of fresh coffee being made in the mornings. She was frying baking and eggs, toast. I can hear the sounds of neighborhood kids playing outside of their houses and the sounds of the ice cream truck.

Untitled

Edgar Castan

People ask me why I take my dog everywhere. You see, my dog, Maya, is a ten-year-old sweet and friendly pit bull girl who has been with me for her entire life. She rides with me in the back of my car, sometimes in the passenger seat, while I work my food delivery job during lunch time, nights, and weekends. She likes to put her head out the window and take short sniffs. She never sticks her entire head out. I believe she is introverted but never too shy to meet new people. I try to imagine what it is that her nose is smelling. A squirrel? A dog's butt? A grilled steak? I like to tell people that she keeps me company. She is my partner and my family and I need to protect her from a loved one at home who has threatened to let her loose in the street if I don't send her money to feed her heroin addiction. I bring her to protect her.

BIOS

Jamiece Adams is a 2019 Lambda Literary fellow and teacher based in Chicago. She earned her MFA in fiction at Columbia College Chicago. Recently she worked on a multidisciplinary project, *Take Care*, which examined the roles of intimacy and correspondence, her poem is featured in the limited-edition artist book. Currently, she's working on a collection of short stories. Some of these pieces have been published in *Hair Trigger, Rabbit: Nonfiction Poetry Journal*, *The Lindenwood Review,* and forthcoming in the *2019 Lambda Literary Anthology of Emerging LGBTQ+ writers.*

A Chicago-native, **J. A. Bernstein** is the author of a novel, *Rachel's Tomb* (New Issues, 2019), which won the A.W.P. Award Series and Hackney Prizes; and a chapbook, *Desert Castles* (Southern Indiana Review, 2019), which won the Wilhelmus Prize. His stories, poems, and essays have appeared in about seventy-five journals and anthologies, including *Shenandoah*, *Boston Review*, *Chicago Quarterly*, *Tin House*, and *Kenyon Review*, and won the Gunyon Prize at *Crab Orchard Review*. A husband and father of three, he teaches in the Center for Writers at the University of Southern Mississippi and is the fiction editor of *Tikkun Magazine*.

David Bontumasi's stories have previously been featured in *Hypertext Magazine*, as well as *Poached Hare,* the *Write Launch, Black Mirror,* the *RavensPerch* and others. His novella, *Of This Earth*, was set in Sicily and Michigan in the 1920s, and he's hard at work on a collection of short stories. Born and raised in Flint, Michigan, David lives just outside Chicago with his wife and two sons. Visit him at *davidbontumasi. com*

Alexis Bowe is an emerging writer from the suburbs of Chicago. She enjoys writing from a strong female perspective, and many of her stories touch on women's issues. In addition to writing short stories, she is also in the process of writing her first novel. When she isn't writing, Alexis enjoys traveling all over the country to attend concerts and music festivals. Her work can be found in *Hair Trigger* and *Hair Trigger 2.0.*

Fleda Brown's *The Woods Are On Fire: New & Selected Poems*, was chosen by Ted Kooser for his University of Nebraska poetry series in 2017. She has nine previous collections of poems. Her work has appeared three times in *The Best American Poetry* and has won a Pushcart Prize, the Felix Pollak Prize, the Philip Levine Prize, and the Great Lakes Colleges New Writer's Award, and has twice been a finalist for the National Poetry Series. Her memoir, *Driving With Dvorak,* was published in 2010 by the University of Nebraska Press. She is professor emerita at the University of Delaware, where she directed the Poets in the Schools program. She was poet laureate of Delaware from 2001-07. She now lives with her husband, Jerry Beasley, in Traverse City, Michigan, and is on the faculty of the Rainier Writing Workshop, a low-residency MFA program in Tacoma, Washington.

Ana Castillo is a celebrated and distinguished poet, novelist, short story writer, essayist, editor, playwright, translator and independent scholar. Castillo was born and raised in Chicago. Among her award winning, best selling titles: novels include *So Far From God, The Guardians* and Peel *My Love like an Onion*, among other poetry: *I Ask the Impossible.* Her novel, *Sapogonia* was a New York Times Notable Book of the Year. In 2014 Dr. Castillo held the Lund-Gil Endowed Chair at Dominican University, River Forest, IL and served on the faculty with Bread Loaf Summer Program (Middlebury College) in 2015 and 2016. She also held the first Sor uana Inés de la Cruz Endowed Chair at DePaul University, The Martin Luther King, Jr Distinguished Visiting Scholar post at M.I.T. , among other posts. Ana Castillo holds a Ph.D., University of Bremen, Germany in American Studies and an honorary doctorate from Colby College. Her most recent titles, *Give it to Me* (a novel) and *Black Dove: Mamá, Mi'jo, and Me* (personal essays/memoir) received LAMBDA Awards. In 2018, Dr. Castillo received PEN Oakland Reginald Lockett Lifetime Achievement Award.

Giano Cromley is the author of the novel *The Last Good Halloween,* and the short story collection *What We Build Upon the Ruins*, both of which were finalists for the High Plains Book Award. His writing has appeared in the *Chicago Tribune*, *The Threepenny Review*, *Literal Latte*, and the German edition of *Le Monde diplomatique*, among others. He moonlights as an assistant editor for *Identity Theory*. And he has received an Artists Fellowship from the Illinois Arts Council. He is the chair of the Communications Department at Kennedy-King College, and he lives on the South Side of Chicago with his wife and two dogs.

Meredith Counts is a Michigan writer and archives student with an MFA from the Fiction Writing Department at Columbia College Chicago. Her writing and reviews have recently appeared in Foreword, Portage Magazine, Quail Bell, Traverse, the Detroit Metro Times, Chicago Literati, and BUST. She is one of the founding editors of Dead Housekeeping and is co-editing a book by Detroit poet Jim Gustafson, who was her uncle.

Originally hailing from Alabama, **Miranda Dennis** studied at Hollins University and the University of Massachusetts-Amherst's MFA Program for Poets and Writers. Her poetry has previously been published in *Meridian*, *storySouth*, *Jellyfish* magazine, *Cold Mountain Review*, and *Watershed Review*. Additionally, her essays have appeared in *Quail Bell Magazine* and *Granta* online. She works in product marketing for a digital advertising firm in Manhattan and lives with a fat tuxedo cat in upper Manhattan.

Margaret Erhart's work has appeared in *The New York Times*, *Christian Science Monitor*, and *The Best American Spiritual Writing 2005*. Her commentaries have aired on NPR. She won the Milkweed National Fiction Prize and was a finalist for an Amazon Breakthrough Novel Award. She lives and works in Flagstaff, Arizona. You can find her at www.margareterhart.com

Betsy Finesilver Haberl writes fiction and nonfiction. She received her MFA in Creative Writing from Northwestern University. She is also a curator for Sunday Salon Chicago, one of the city's longest-running literary reading series. She was born and raised in northeastern Wisconsin, but now lives in Evanston, Illinois, with her family.

Steve Hughes Steve Hughes is the writer and publisher of Detroit's longest-running zine *Stupor*. He is also the author of two collections, *Stupor: A Treasury of True Stories* (Stupor House, 2011), funded by the Kresge Foundation, and *STIFF* (Wayne State University Press, 2018). In 2011, he began producing the potluck/literary series called The Good Tyme Writers Buffet. Hughes lives in Hamtramck Michigan and continues to collect stories at local watering holes for forthcoming issues of *Stupor*.

billy lombardo is a writer, editor, and teacher from Chicago, Illinois. billy is the author of *The Logic of a Rose: Chicago Stories, The Man with Two Arms,* and *Meanwhile, Roxy Mourns*. His novel, *How to Hold a Woman* will be re-issued by Tortoise Books as *Morning Will Come* in January 2021. His most recent work has been published in *Hypertext Magazine*, Ireland's *HCE Review*, The *Tishman Review, Tikkun Magazine, The Chicago Reader, The Chicago Tribune*, and *Triquarterly.* billy is the 2011 Nelson Algren Fiction Award winner. He is currently at work on the *House of Fiction Deconstructed for the Apprentice Writer*. billy is also the founder and managing editor of *Polyphony Lit,* a student-run, international literary magazine for high school writers and editors *www.polyphonylit.org*. An international staff of two hundred high school students comment on every one of more than 2,000 submissions that come to *Polyphony Lit* from more than 70 countries so far. billy can be reached through his writing and editing, business, *Writing Pros/e,* at *www.writingprose.org*. He lives in Chicago's Albany Park neighborhood.

Rebecca McClanahan has published ten books, most recently *The Tribal Knot: A Memoir of Family, Community, and a Century of Change*. Her work has appeared in *Best American Essays, Best American Poetry, Boulevard, Georgia Review, Kenyon Review, Gettysburg Review, Southern Review, The Sun*, and numerous anthologies. Recipient of the Wood Prize from *Poetry* Magazine, two Pushcart Prizes, the Carter Prize for the Essay, and the Glasgow Award in Nonfiction for her suite of essays, *The Riddle Song and Other Rememberings*, she teaches in the MFA programs of Queens University and Rainier Writing Workshop. Red Hen Press will publish her memoir-in-essays *In the Key of New York City* in 2020.

John McNally is the author of ten books, including the novel *The Book of Ralph* and, more recently, *The Promise of Failure: One Writer's Perspective on Not Succeeding.* "The Devil in the Details" is from a recently completed story collection titled *The Fear of Everything.* He is presently writing feature screenplays for the Norwegian film company Evil Doghouse. A native of the southwest Chicago suburb Burbank, John now lives in Lafayette, Louisiana, where is he is Writer-in-Residence and the Dr. Doris Meriwether/BORSF Professor in English at the University of Louisiana at Lafayette.

B.L. Makiefsky was the winner of the 2012 Michigan Writers Cooperative Press chapbook contest, for his short story collection "Fathers And Sons." His work has appeared, or will appear, in the Detroit Free Press, Fan Magazine, Dunes Review, Thoughtful Dog, Pithead Chapel, Brilliant Flash Fiction, Fiction Southeast and Dreamers Magazine. He was an analyst for the Michigan Dept. of Health and Human Services before retiring in 2018. He lives and writes in Traverse City, Michigan.

David Medina has authored four short stories, so far. In addition to "Pleased To Meet You", they include "Sofie The Warrior Queen" (34th Parallel Literary Review, 2018), "The Tickle In His Tail" (Raconteur Fiction Anthology, 1995), and "Sweatshop" (El Boletin Magazine, 1993). He spent the bulk of his career as a news writer, editor and columnist at five different newspapers. He has dedicated himself to full time fiction writing since 2016 and takes master classes at the Writers Studio in New York City.

Simone Muench is the author of six full-length books, including *Wolf Centos* (Sarabande, 2014) and *Orange Crush* (Sarabande, 2010). Her recent, *Suture*, includes sonnets written with Dean Rader (Black Lawrence, 2017). She is an editor of *They Said: A Multi-Genre Anthology of Contemporary Collaborative Writing* (Black Lawrence, 2018) and creator of the HB Sunday Reading Series in Chicago. Additionally, she serves as faculty advisor for *Jet Fuel Review* and as a senior poetry editor for *Tupelo Quarterly.*

In August, **Mike Puican**'s debut book of poetry, *Central Air,* will be released by Northwestern Press. He has had poems in *Poetry, Michigan Quarterly Review,* and *New England Review,* among others. He won the 2004 Tia Chucha Press Chapbook Contest for his chapbook, *30 Seconds.* Mike was a member of the 1996 Chicago Slam Team, and is past president and long-time board member of the Guild Literary Complex in Chicago. Currently he teaches poetry to incarcerated and formerly incarcerated individuals at the Federal Metropolitan Correctional Center and St. Leonard's House.

Lillie Rice is a native Chicagoan and recent graduate of Sarah Lawrence College. Her visual art has been published in the *Sarah Lawrence Review.* She continues to read and write poetry while living in New York City.

Greg Halvorsen Schreck's photography projects are connected to portraiture, human rights issues, landscapes, and environmental concerns. His most recent exhibition, in 2018, reflected his months in Guatemala with the Quiche Maya. It consisted of portraits and a visual interpretation of the Popol Vuh, the Mayan creation story. The photo on the cover is of Willy Barreno, the Director of Desgua, an organization dedicated to the re-migration of Guatemalans, located in Quetzaltenango (aka Xela), Guatemala. Schreck teaches photography and other art classes at Wheaton College, near Chicago. His undergraduate degree is from Rochester Institute of Technology where he studied both commercial and fine art photography. Schreck completed his graduate work at New York University and the International Center of Photography. He lives in Wheaton, Illinois with his family. You can see examples of his work at gregschreckphotography.com

Jesse Sensibar's work has appeared in *The Tishman Review, Stoneboat Journal, Waxwing,* and others. His short fiction was shortlisted for the Bath Flash Fiction Award and the Wilda Hearne Flash Fiction Prize. His first book, *Blood in the Asphalt: Prayers from the Highway,* was published in 2018 by Tolsun Press and shortlisted for the Eric Hoffer Book Award. You can find him at jessesensibar.com.

Shawn Shiflett is an Associate Professor in the English and Creative Writing Department at Columbia College Chicago. His debut novel, *Hidden Place* (*Akashic Books,* 2004), received rave reviews from newspapers, literary magazines, and *Connie Martinson Talks*

Books (national cable television, UK and Ireland). Library Journal included *Hidden Place* in "Summer Highs, Fall Firsts," a 2004 list of most successful debuts. He was awarded an Illinois Arts Council Fellowship for his work and was a three-time Finalist for the James novel-in-progress contest, sponsored by the Heekin Group Foundation. New City Newspaper elected Shiflett to their Chicago Lit 50 list, an annual ranking of top figures in the Chicago Literary scene. His essay, "The Importance of Reading to Your Writing" (*Creative Writing Studies*, UK) was published in 2013. His novel, *Hey, Liberal!* (*Chicago Review Press*, 2016), a story about a white boy going to a predominately African American high school in Chicago during the late 1960's, has received acclaim from *Booklist, The Chicago Tribune, Kirkus Review, Newcity Lit, Windy City Review*, Mary Mitchell (*Chicago Sun-Times*), Rick Kogan (*WGN Radio*), and others. Excerpts from Shiflett's novels and short stories can be found in *Hypertext Magazine*, various issues of *F Magazine*, and other literary journals. In 2018, he performed his oral story performance "How My Yo-Yo Could Have Gotten me Killed," and in 2019 he performed "Oriole Park, from White America to Multicultural America." He is on the Chicago Writers Association Board of Directors. Currently, he is working on a non-fiction, multicultural project: collecting oral stories concerning race. Several pieces from his work-in-progress *My Secret Lives (a murmur of dreams)*, will be forthcoming in Hypertext Magazine, fall 2019. Shiflett lives with his wife, a couple of step-cats, and an English setters named Higgins. *Shawnshiflett.com*

Jackie K. White is a professor at Lewis University and a faculty advisor for *Jet Fuel Review*. She was just named the 2019 winner of the Reid H. Montgomery Distinguished Service Award by the CMA. Recent poems appear in *Tupelo Quarterly*, along with collaborative poems published or forthcoming in *Pleiades, The Journal, Isthmus, Posit, Bennington Review, Hypertext,* and *Cincinnati Review*. She has published three chapbooks, and served as an assistant editor for the collaborative anthology, *They Said*.

Michael Williamson grew up in Mississippi and Kentucky. These days, he lives in Chicago with his wife and his cat.

Jeremy T. Wilson is the author of the short story collection *Adult Teeth* (Tortoise Books) and a former winner of the *Chicago Tribune's* Nelson Algren Award for short fiction. His stories have appeared in literary magazines such as *The Carolina Quarterly*, *The Florida Review*, *The Masters Review*, *Sonora Review*, *Third Coast* and other publications. He holds an MFA from Northwestern University and teaches creative writing at The Chicago High School for the Arts.

Colophon

Hypertext Review was produced on an Apple Macbook Pro using Adobe InDesign. The cover and photo pages were produced on an Apple iMac using Adobe Photoshop. Files were submitted to KDP, via electronic submission.

The cover image was provided by the artist in digital format and submitted to KDP via electronic submission.

The cover copy is Omnes Regular and Arial.

Body copy is Bookmania Regular 11 point. Titles are in Omnes Regular 28 point, subtitles are in Omnes Regular 20 point, author names are in Omnes Regular 16 point, footers are in Omnes Regular 8 point.

Paper stock for cover is 55# (90 GSM) white paper stock with matte finish.

Paper stock for the interior is 60 lb. white 444ppi.

Print run: on demand

Made in the USA
Monee, IL
10 November 2019

16604645R10116